BRIDES
WEDDING BOOK

BRIDES
WEDDING BOOK

ELIZABETH HILLIARD
for BRIDES AND SETTING UP HOME

CONDÉ NAST BOOKS
London   Sydney   Auckland   Johannesburg

For
William and Hugh
Heather and David

Edited by Cindy Richards
Designed by Sara Robin
Picture research by Shona Wood

First published in 1992 by Condé Nast Publications Ltd.,
an imprint of the Random Century Group Ltd.,
Random Century House, 20 Vauxhall Bridge Road,
London SW1V 2SA

Random Century Australia (Pty) Ltd., 20 Alfred Street,
Milsons Point, Sydney, New South Wales 2061, Australia

Random Century New Zealand Ltd., 18 Poland Road,
Glenfield, Auckland 10, New Zealand

Random Century South Africa (Pty) Ltd., PO Box 337,
Bergvlei 2012, South Africa

Set in Bembo by
Rowland Phototypesetting Ltd.,
Bury St Edmunds, Suffolk
Printed and bound in Italy by
New Interlitho Spa, Milan

A catalogue record for this book is
available from the British Library

ISBN 0 09 177015 7

CONTENTS

ACKNOWLEDGEMENTS

Elizabeth Hilliard would like to thank the following for their contribution of original material from *Brides and Setting Up Home* magazine:

Tim Atkin
Pamela Blount
Sandra Boler
Mark Cockerton
Lottie Johansson
John Keegan
Lucy Keegan
Susanne Keegan
Anne Longden
Susannah Moss
Sarah Powys Maurice
Christina Probert Jones
Christian Rucker
Julia Sherbrooke
Joanna Slaughter
Polly Toynbee
Roger Voss
Sarah Waghorn
Adrienne Wilkinson
Madeleine Youlten

All *Brides and Setting Up Home* magazine's contributors
and editorial staff of the last six years.

She would also like to thank the following for their generous help and supply of information: Hilary Arnold; The Very Reverend William Baddeley; Mr Johnny and Lady Lilias Bell; Jeffery Blumenfeld, Jewish Marriage Council; Stephen Borton, Faculty Office; Felicity Bryan; Valerie Buckingham; Benjamin Cooper; The Reverend Patrick Craig; The Family Planning Association; Mrs Paul Farmiloe; Fillans Antiques; Mr and Mrs David Hilliard; Susi Hornung; Mrs David Jackson; Miss Rosemary Lomax-Simpson; Major and Mrs Francis Lukas; Meredith MacArdle, British Humanist Society; Charlotte Molesworth; Jane Packer; The Very Reverend Archimandrite Sofronios Papadopoulos; Office of Population Census and Surveys; Nigel Sargeant, Passport Agency; Mrs Max Selka; William Selka; Simon Sheard; and the many people whose weddings she has attended over the years as well as all the people who helped organise her own.

FOREWORD

There can be no day more eagerly awaited, no day anticipated with more excitement than your wedding day. This is the culmination of every bride's dream, the day she has planned in every tiny detail. From the moment when you accept your lover's proposal you set in motion one of the happiest events of both of your lives.

As I discovered from experience it is also one of the busiest times you will ever know with seemingly endless things to do, lists to be drawn up, people to be consulted and an infinite number of decisions to be made.

Planning can be the greatest pleasure. The dress, flowers, music, the choice of wedding service – all are part of the ritual of life's most glorious celebration. The individual touches you add to your wedding plans are what go to make your wedding day uniquely yours and the happiest day of your life.

The months and weeks leading up to their wedding are of the greatest importance to every engaged couple. Don't forget in the midst of all the excitement that its your fiancé's wedding day too and it's important to get the balance right.

In this book you will find the answers to all your questions, a constant source of advice, ideas and inspiration. Whether for major decisions or minor details, colour, price, timing, order, who walks where and who pays for what, the finer points of etiquette or what to pack for your honeymoon, I believe this book will be your treasured guide.

SANDRA BOLER, Editor
Brides and Setting Up Home

INTRODUCTION

Congratulations on your engagement! You and your fiancé have made the momentous decision to get married. Now you face the daunting task of organising the wedding itself, the most thrilling day of your life. People say it's like being Queen for a day: everything is arranged in the way you want it, and all eyes are on you.

The organisation will take several months because a wedding is such a complex event. You may feel overwhelmed at the prospect and think to yourself: 'What I need is a good friend who has herself been married and who therefore knows the ins and outs of organising a wedding . . . someone who loves weddings and has a fund of bright ideas . . . someone who will help make my wedding really special and individual.' That's the point of this book – to be your friend and guide, making the task of organising the perfect wedding easier and more exciting.

It's also about choices. The style of your wedding will reflect your character and tastes. You may have a clear idea of exactly what you want, or you many have an open mind; you might want six close friends at a short register office or religious ceremony, or 600 relations and friends at a cathedral; a sophisticated city wedding in winter, a simple country event in summer.

Whatever suits you, it will seem like there are a million decisions and choices to be made. What to wear to make the most of your colouring and figure; who to invite and not invite, and where to seat them; what colour theme and type of flowers to have and where to put them; what food and drink to offer; when to cut the cake; and so on . . . Other people will have views, and there are practical considerations like cost, but ultimately the choices are yours. Remember this is your and your fiancé's wedding, not your mother's or anyone else's, however much valued support they give you and however great their contribution to the event.

One of the first choices you will have to make is where to be married. According to current statistics, roughly two-thirds of religious weddings, and about a third of all weddings, take place in Anglican churches. Special sections on The Service and Music take this into account. But this book is designed to be useful whatever kind of wedding and celebrations you choose, be it a register office ceremony followed by a drinks party, a Jewish wedding in a synagogue followed by a formal dinner and dancing, or a humanist celebration in the open air, followed by a hop in the local village hall and a firework display.

On a purely practical level, decision-making is more fun when you feel confident and well-informed. If you know what questions to ask when you talk to professionals such as caterers, photographers, florists and the minister or officiant, you are more likely to get the results you want, and at the right price.

The pictures in these pages offer a wealth of ideas to inspire every aspect of the look of your wedding. The text is packed with information and useful tips on every detail of wedding organisation and etiquette. It also guides you through more personal but equally significant matters like getting on with your in-laws, choosing a form of contraception, and the importance of talking to your fiancé about your expectations of marriage itself.

Pre-wedding nerves are famous. Almost every bride has them, and a touch of stage fright rarely does any harm. But if worries persist and you have serious doubts, you should think carefully about the sort of wedding you want, and perhaps about marrying at all. A big, glamorous wedding may be what you always envisaged, but a small low-key affair might suit your nature better. Don't lose sight of what it's essentially about: you are getting married in order to share your life with the man you love, not in order to have the wedding. If the problem is more serious and your nerves are a signal that you are not doing the right thing in marrying this person, it is better to cancel the wedding. Don't be steamrollered by the enormity of the arrangements or the advanced stage of the wedding preparations.

Weddings are a focus for boundless love and good will, and yours should be no exception. I hope you will use this book to help take the stress out of the organisation and preparations so that your wedding day is the happiest day of your life and a joy to look back on in years to come. Remember, it's your day – make it how you want it, don't worry, and enjoy yourself.

Good luck!

1
BEGINNINGS

THE PROPOSAL

'Will you marry me?' must be some of the most heavily loaded words in the English language. The entire future lives of at least two people rest upon them and upon the reply. The proposal, whether long-expected or sudden, can produce an electric tingle and the minutes and hours after an acceptance can seem unreal. Perhaps it's difficult to believe this has really happened; probably it's impossible to get your new future together into focus. Quite rightly, mundane practicalities do not enter your thoughts, for this is a time for dreams, a time of pure magic.

A proposal is the crystallisation of feelings and thoughts which might have been very powerful but have not until now taken a specific form. Queen Victoria asked Prince Albert but usually it's the other way around and the man who does the proposing. This is because, traditionally, he is inviting his future wife to take his name and status (which is why Queen Victoria reversed the roles – her position was the greater). Today it is still generally true that the man is expected to be the material provider if the couple decide to have children. When he asks, 'Will you marry me?' he is declaring his willingness to adopt this responsibility. An offhand 'I think it's about time we got married,' doesn't have quite the same impact. One important difference is that it doesn't require the girl to stop and think about whether this is what she really wants, or give her the opportunity to declare her commitment too. After all, in the long term the man may bear the greater economic burden, but marriage may not change his outward life very much, while

the woman's is quite likely to change radically. She may have to move to the place where he and possibly his family live and work. If they have children it is she who suffers the discomfort of pregnancy and childbirth and generally she who thereafter provides or organises decades of childcare, food and clothing. All this is often in addition to her job or career, and in spite of greater recognition of the equality of the sexes. Marriage is no meal ticket for women, whatever the male chauvinist jokers would have us believe.

The days are long past when a man really needed the girl's parents' approval before considering himself engaged to be married. As a matter of courtesy, however, the custom of asking the bride-to-be's father continues. If, for a large part of her life her parents have provided their daughter with a home and the necessities of living, including perhaps the education which set her on the road to being able to make a significant financial contribution to the marriage, it is only civil for the potential son-in-law to acknowledge this and declare his recognition of the seriousness of the commitment. All this doesn't need actually to be said; the very fact of asking says it all. The request also offers a formal opportunity for the fiancé to explain himself to her father, financially or otherwise, if either party wishes this. The formality of the moment is especially helpful if either man would find it hard to raise the subject without it, or if the fiancé is barely known to the girl's parents. Questions can happily be asked and answered which at other times might seem impertinent.

The proposal and the business of asking the bride-to-be's father are also, quite simply, part of the enjoyable ritual of getting married, ritual which helps make us feel secure and happy. They mark the first steps in the run-up to the event of the marriage and, once they are complete, you and your parents can then get down to the practicalities of organising the wedding. Many couples have engagement photographs taken when the engagement is to be of any length or where families are scattered over the country and haven't met both partners, or just because it's fun to have them. The photographs can be snapshots taken by a friend or formal studio portraits in colour or black and white. They will remind you of the beginning of some of the happiest (and busiest) days of your life.

REAL-LIFE PROPOSALS

The proposal which marks the start of your engagement is a moment you will never forget and, if he has an ounce of romance in him, a man's choice of timing and surroundings will reflect this. 'Do come up on the battlements for a walk . . .' said Matthew, a young doctor, to the girl he had been going out with for over a year. The occasion was a dance at Stirling Castle in Scotland in the middle of winter. 'No, it's much too cold,' said Antonia, but seeing he was so very keen she should go, she relented. They went out on to the battlements in the snow and he asked her to marry him.

He took Antonia completely by surprise but so did the man who thought that after several weeks of the same heavy (he thought) hint, the girl he'd been seeing must know what he was talking about. 'For weeks he kept bringing up the subject of jewels and precious stones. What kind of stone did I like best? Did I like old or new jewellery? I had no particular interest in jewels and I could not understand his fixation. It was even beginning to annoy me rather. Finally, one evening we were doing the washing-up and he asked me again if I liked diamonds or had any other favourite stone, and I said to him: "What is all this about?" He stopped drying up and looked at me and said, "Do you really not know what I'm talking about?" And suddenly I realised. I went bright red and said, "Stop! We can't possibly have this conversation in the kitchen over the washing-up." So we dropped it all instantly and went into the sitting room and he actually did it. He went down on one knee and asked me to marry him, there and then.' The ring they finally chose was an amethyst.

Peter already had the ring when he asked Debbie to marry him and, as they had chosen it together, she knew he was going to propose. 'He had asked me years ago, soon after we first got together, and I said no, and he didn't mention it again, not once, until then. Yes, I was getting a bit impatient: I thought he would ask me the previous autumn when we were on holiday but he didn't, he now tells me, because he was afraid I would say no again.'

It seems generally to be true that a man doesn't like to propose on holiday for fear of a refusal which might put the rest of the holiday under a black cloud. Elizabeth and Richard had been on holiday in Brittany not long before he proposed and Elizabeth admits she half-expected him to ask her to

marry him there. Instead he waited until their return, and it was a completely unconnected event which prompted his proposal. One Friday he was offered substantial promotion at work and, in his excitement, it all tumbled out together when he saw Elizabeth that evening. 'He burst out with the news about his work, then said will you marry me almost in the same breath.'

A prize for a truly romantic proposal, with a complicated, well-planned and expensive build-up (and one that breaks the not-on-holiday rule) goes to Mick. 'It was November,' explains Miranda. 'He insisted we go to Norfolk for the weekend which made me cross because I had to rearrange my work and take a day off which was inconvenient. I left a suitcase of winter woollies and clothes suitable for the country at home and Mick met me with it later. We got on the underground in London at Earl's Court and I said that this wasn't the way to go to Norfolk. He said, "Don't ask questions," which was mysterious. Before I knew it we were at Heathrow and on a plane to **Venice**! We went to the hotel and then out to dinner. Later, I discovered he'd unpacked and repacked my suitcase with clothes suitable for Venice – this is a man who usually hasn't a clue about clothes. Anyway, we sat down in the restaurant and the waiter asked what we'd like to drink. Mick said, "It depends on the answer to this question." He turned to me and said, "Will you marry me?" It was a total surprise. I absolutely wasn't expecting it. And I said, jokingly, "Do we get champagne if I say yes?" And he said yes so how could I say no.'

ENGAGEMENT AND WEDDING RINGS

Engagement rings fall into three broad types: antique, modern, and specially commissioned. The subject of antique rings is a huge one in itself. In order to be sure of what you are buying (whether antique or modern), it is important to buy from a knowledgeable, reputable dealer, especially since rings made before 1975 are not necessarily hallmarked. Antique rings can be less expensive than modern ones because the costs involved in manufacture are higher today. Commissioning your own ring can be exciting and, if you already have the stones, not necessarily more expensive than buying.

The tradition of giving a diamond engagement ring is believed to have started in 1477 when Maximilian of Hapsburg gave one to his fiancée, Mary of Burgundy. Wedding rings have an even longer history. The Ancient Egyptians are the first civilisation we know used rings as adornment and symbols of wealth, a tradition continued and expanded in Europe by the Romans. Today one of the early excitements of engagement is the selecting and wearing of a jewelled ring. Choosing it may be among the first things you do as an engaged couple and, once on your finger, the ring will remind you of this and all the other precious times you have spent and will spend together. It is a love token for all the world to see and it indicates your status as an attached person, almost married. The choosing is a deliciously romantic moment but, as with all aspects of getting married (and indeed marriage itself), it is as well to have the practical considerations clear in your mind.

The first of these is money. You (or your fiancé) need to have a budget, within which you want to get the very best stones your money can buy. This means going to a reputable jeweller who is a member of the National Association of Goldsmiths, St Dunstan's House, 2 Carey Lane, London EC2V 8AB (tel: 071 726 4374). If you ring them they will give you lists of members in your area. A good jeweller will be discreet about money, asking your fiancé out of your hearing what price range he has in mind, just in case it is to be a secret. If the jeweller lacks tact your fiancé can say, 'I'd like to tell you in private,' and take the jeweller to one side. Whatever the budget, you are certain to find a beautiful ring to suit you.

The next consideration is your hands. Take a good look at them, bearing in mind that delicate rings look best on slender fingers while heavier hands best offset larger, bolder designs. Short fingers are flattered by a single oval or marquisite cut stone (see page 19). Your personal style is important too. If you are an informal person you may prefer a simpler ring, perhaps a gold band incorporating diamonds or coloured gems rather than a more traditional setting. Remember that if you like wearing jumpers a large or upstanding ring can be impractical as it is likely to catch. Be aware that fashion affects the style of rings, as it does most other things. If you want a modern ring look for a design that will age gracefully with the passing years, although it is possible to have the gems reset later. Finally, don't forget that your engagement ring will be worn next to your wedding ring, so their appearance and metals (see page 18) should be compatible.

Make sure your hands look their best when you go to choose your ring, with clean, neat nails so that you feel relaxed and confident. Don't be embarrassed to try on lots of rings in different styles, including some which don't look quite right in the tray – they may look wonderful on your hand. You might have thought you wanted an antique ring but instead fall in love with a modern design. Leave plenty of time and take your time; don't be rushed by your fiancé or the jeweller and don't make an instant decision if there is any doubt in your mind. There are always other jewellers and other rings.

If you really cannot find what you want, or if the idea of a ring

BIRTHSTONES

JANUARY GARNET *Truth and faithfulness*	FEBRUARY AMETHYST *Serenity*	MARCH AQUAMARINE *Courage*
APRIL DIAMOND *Innocence and harmony*	MAY EMERALD *Love and success*	JUNE PEARL *Purity*
JULY RUBY *Contentment*	AUGUST PERIDOT *Inspiration*	SEPTEMBER SAPPHIRE *Repentance*
OCTOBER OPAL *Good fortune*	NOVEMBER TOPAZ *Faithfulness*	DECEMBER TURQUOISE *Prosperity*

that is exclusively yours appeals, it is possible to commission a jeweller to make your ring (see below). Occasionally it may be a matter not of choosing a ring or commissioning it, but of being offered one which has been in your fiancé's family for generations and which they expect you to wear. Often such a ring is finer and more valuable than one your fiancé could afford to buy and, of course, it signifies that you are on the point of becoming not only his wife but also an important member of his family. On the other hand, the offer can be a strain if the ring is not a stone or style you like. If possible you should accept it because it is important to your fiancé and it could hurt him if you rejected this family heirloom. The ring may mean more to him than anything that can be bought in the shops. It will also be, and be seen to be, a bond between you and your future in-laws. If you reject it, you may upset them as well as him at a time when you are just beginning to build a relationship with them. Depending on the length and strength of the tradition attached to the ring, it may be possible to refuse it graciously, perhaps by introducing the idea that you had set your heart on a ruby rather than a sapphire, for example, or if your fiancé sees that its size and shape clearly do not suit your hand.

The giving and receiving of a ring or rings is a vital part of the religious service of marriage, with the ring's unbroken circle signifying the never ending love of God as well as the marriage contract between man and woman. Gold is the preferred material for wedding rings which, increasingly frequently, are worn by men as well as by women. Also popular are gem-set wedding rings, many quite elaborate and in some cases acting both as engagement and wedding ring.

The popularity of gold is not surprising. It will never tarnish, cannot be destroyed and its natural, warm colour can be varied by alloying it with a variety of metals such as copper, nickel and palladium to produce a rich rainbow of shades of yellow, white, red and green. The proportion of gold in your wedding ring is measured in carats: 24-carat gold is completely pure while 22-carat has 916.6 parts of gold in 1,000; 18 has 750 parts gold in 1,000 and 9-carat has 375 in 1,000. Eighteen and 9 are the most popular, 18 in particular combining richness of colour with hardness for durability. An alternative to gold is platinum, whose silver colour combines well with diamonds and blue-toned stones. Whatever the material, you can have the inside of your wedding ring engraved

with the date of your wedding, both your initials and even a special message. Instead of buying a wedding ring, another option is wearing one already in the family – there is no superstition attached to this unless the previous owner is known to have had an unhappy marriage.

Diamonds are the most popular stone for engagement rings, used either alone or combined with coloured gems. Four important elements govern the quality and value of a diamond (see 'How to Choose a Diamond' chart).

COMMISSIONING A RING

Commissioning your engagement or wedding ring can be much more expensive than buying, especially if you do not already have the stones you want incorporated into it, perhaps in an old ring or rings whose setting you don't like. The new ring, however, will be unique, created specifically for your character and style, your colouring and hands.

Before commissioning a ring from a jeweller, check his credentials and see previous designs he has created. For reassurance about his skill and reliability, ask to be put in touch with the owners of other rings he has made. Try on some of his rings, and others in other jewellers' shops, to help you decide what looks good on you and what you want. The designer's job will be made easier if you have previously thought about:
▶ budget
▶ the stones or colour of stones
▶ the size and design of all parts of your ring, including the shank (under your finger) and the mount (on top, holding the stone(s))

The commission will involve four stages before you collect the finished ring.
▶ A discussion of what you want to spend, the type of design and stones. If the designer is present he may do some rough sketches
▶ Finished designs. If you decide against going ahead you will probably be asked to pay for these drawings.
▶ Examination of a choice of stones. Ask the jeweller to tell you in detail what the quality is of the stones he is showing you, and ask to see them laid on white paper so you can see their true colour (perhaps take a sheet of white paper or handkerchief with you). A

HOW TO CHOOSE A DIAMOND

CARAT

One carat equals one-fifth of a gram. Each carat is 100 points, so a diamond of 25 points is a quarter of a carat. In general, the larger the diamond the more valuable it is, and a large diamond is worth more than two of an equal combined weight. Two diamonds of the same size can vary greatly in value, however, depending on their quality.

CLARITY

A flawless diamond is extremely rare. Most contain tiny flaws, called 'inclusions', which occur naturally as the diamond forms from pure, crystallised carbon, and which make each stone unique. Fewer flaws mean greater value but tiny ones do not affect a diamond's strength or beauty.

COLOUR

Colourless diamonds are very rare and costly. Most have a slight yellow tint which diminishes the value as it becomes stronger. Unusual pink, green and blue diamonds, however, are known as 'fancies' and are collectors' items.

CUT

In its raw state, a diamond looks like a dull glass pebble. The cut transforms it, minimising the flaws and maximising the amount of light refracted and reflected through the stone from one carefully angled facet to another. Of all cuts, the brilliant is the most popular.

dark velvet background can make them look finer than they are. Ask to see them mounted in plasticine in the arrangement you have agreed

▶ A fitting and any final adjustments

You may also want to see and try on the mount before the stones are set into it.

HALLMARKS

There should be five marks on the inside or side of a gold ring, certifying that it has been tested at one of the four Assay offices. Since 1975 the Hallmarking Act has made it illegal to sell any piece of precious metal in Britain without first submitting it for assaying and marking. Jewellery made before then is not subject to the act so old or antique rings may not carry a hallmark.

The Sponsor's Mark is the initial of the article's manufacturer.
The Quality Mark is a crown, proving the jewellery is gold (platinum has a cross and orb) and has been hallmarked in the UK.
The Standard Mark gives the carat quality figures and shows the metal content is not less than the standard indicated.
The Assay Office Mark identifies the office where the piece was tested and marked. The symbols are an anchor for Birmingham, a rose for Sheffield, a castle for Edinburgh and a leopard for London.
The Date Letter indicates the year in which the ring was made. The letter for 1987, for example, was N.

CLEANING AND CARE

Your new rings and their gems need care and attention. Remember to have them insured straightaway. Jewellers recommend a yearly professional clean, check-up and revaluation, but meantime there is plenty you can do. Clean your jewellery regularly, either with a special jewellery-cleaning kit or by brushing gently with a warm solution of liquid detergent before rinsing and patting dry. Alternatively, soak for 30 minutes in a solution of equal parts of household ammonia and cold water. Gently tap and brush to loosen dirt and dip again in the solution – don't rinse. Don't wear your ring for DIY and other dirty or greasy jobs, and don't store it where it can damage or be damaged by other jewellery.

BEING ENGAGED

So it's happened . . . you're engaged to be married. This is a magical time you will both treasure and turn over in your minds through the years to come. And what fun it all is! Bouquets of flowers, letters of congratulation from long-lost friends, parties, and the champagne . . . if you haven't already acquired a taste for this, you soon will. Now that you are officially engaged to be married you can ring up your party hosts (if they don't ring you first) and ask to bring your fiancé along too. You can sit next to each other at dinner parties, at least until you are married and expected to mix. Friends' and relations' good wishes lift you off your feet, into a social whirl that will whisk you to the altar before you know it.

At the same time, your relationship with your fiancé is speeding up too. Engagement is sometimes mistakenly viewed as a kind of full stop. On the contrary, it is a totally fresh start and your relationship is growing and changing faster than ever before. Decisions about everything in your lives become joint – a new and exciting feeling – and these decisions and the way you interact from now on lay the cornerstones of your marriage. You won't have quite the same chance to start your joint life from scratch again so it is important to ensure that you have plenty of private time together to discuss your future, away from the parties and congratulations. There are so many things to cover, including all your expectations, your dreams and aspirations, practical plans and political and religious standpoints. It doesn't make any difference whether you have been living together or not. Being married is quite different . . . it isn't an experiment, it's a master plan for the rest of your life.

The full realisation of what you are undertaking can take its toll, and although celebrating the engagement is fun it can be tiring when combined with planning and organising your wedding day. Most brides will own up to patches of feeling tense and weepy during their engagement. Being ecstatically happy deep down doesn't mean you have to have a smile on your face every second of the day. You need time to yourself as well as time alone with your fiancé, and you shouldn't feel guilty about insisting on it. When you have some peace you will be able to pinpoint the causes of your stress. Exhaustion can be helped easily by making sure you get enough sleep. Aggravation caused by differing views about the religious ceremony or worries about what sort of contraception to use can be alleviated by going to the specialists – your religious adviser or doctor – who will talk to you in confidence. Whatever the problem,

once you start to analyse it and discuss it with your partner, its grip on you begins to weaken. Once engaged, you can feel sufficiently sure of each other's commitment to be relaxed, and brave, about exploring subjects that concern you both.

The fitter you are, the better your body and mind will cope with and enjoy this time. Exercising together is double the fun and makes staying fit a natural, healthy part of your life rather than a dull chore. Start your new plan by stretching out in the morning together or meeting after work to walk home. Take the dog for an evening walk or book a game of tennis. As you get to know each other physically, you will want to concentrate on exercises that make your body look its sexiest and best: side bends to shape your waist, sit-ups to firm your tummy, leg lifts to shape your thighs.

Then there is the question of the style of the wedding itself. You may assume your fiancé envisages exactly the same sort of occasion that you do but you won't know for sure until you ask him. Approach the subject with an open mind – even if you've always dreamed of one kind of wedding, consider other alternatives and think about whether they suit the type of man you are marrying. If he's a countryman, perhaps a farmer, will he feel uncomfortable with a fashionable city wedding? If one of the things you love about him is that he's quiet and unassuming, will he enjoy a large and noisy gathering? You may well arrive back at the idea you started with, and it is after all your day to organise as you please, but you will be even happier with your decision if you take his character and wishes into account.

There is no reason, for instance, why you could not be married at the place where his parents live rather than yours, if they have a particularly lovely garden or house and if this arrangement is agreeable to everyone involved. It might enable you to fulfil your dreams of an English country wedding more readily than if you married from your parents' home. No possibility should be dismissed out of hand. Other people's weddings are the ideal time to take mental notes of what you want (or don't want) yours to be like in style; and if you particularly like the food or flowers, the caterer or florist may be the one you've been searching for to do your wedding.

Besides considering your fiancé, it is obviously vital to involve your parents in these discussions, especially if they will be paying for some or all of the day's celebrations and if your mother is sharing the organisation with you. The subjects you need to cover include: whether you want a civil or religious marriage service; geographic location and exact place of marriage; preferred reception location and numbers; preferred dates (some churches, register offices, halls, caterers and entertainers get booked up very quickly for summer weekends); and the time of day at which the wedding will begin and what will follow in the way of reception, meal, dancing and so on (see pages 40–41). One of the ruling factors in all this is finance, which needs to be gone into in some detail (see pages 32–36).

Another factor is time. The length of your engagement depends upon many things, but six months will give you enough time to organise your wedding so well that you feel totally relaxed and confident on the day. If anything goes wrong (and something little almost always does – it's part of the ritual), it won't be because any of the arrangements were hurried or incomplete. Three months is just enough time to organise a full-scale wedding, but only just, and only if you are prepared to be flexible about locations and dates, or if

you are getting married in an area where there isn't great pressure on the services of clergymen, competent florists and caterers. An engagement is often longer than six months if it begins in the autumn and you want a spring or summer wedding, or if you and your fiancé wish to save up for a home of your own, or for other practical, worldly or religious reasons.

Engagement is a breathing space between the onrush and uncertainties of romance and courtship, and the hoped-for steady growth and stability of marriage. This is the time to air any worries you have about your relationship. We are all only human and we all make mistakes at some point in our lives. Most engaged people, when faced with the enormity of marriage, have pangs and doubts which pass. But if you feel you have definitely made a mistake in becoming engaged to be married to this man, better break off the engagement now than break up a marriage later, when there may be children involved. You won't be the first to end an engagement, even the day before (or the day of) the wedding.

Melanie and Martin knew that engagement can be a strain, so they made sure they had plenty of time alone together in which to relax and talk about the future.

BEING ENGAGED

Caroline and Julian decided to go shopping together for their wedding clothes. Not for her the secret dress that he won't see until she arrives at the altar. She tried on a long, billowy, romantic dress, and a short, sharply elegant dress, but couldn't decide. The short dress showed off her slim figure beautifully and suited her looks and haircut, but the full dress was nearer to her idea of the ideal, traditional wedding gown. Perhaps she could wear something like the short dress to go away in? Anyway, there was no hurry to decide. They moved on to the menswear department. Julian liked the feel and colours of a rich brocaded waistcoat. In the hat department, they both tried on hats for Caroline's going-away outfit, and decided that Julian was irresistible in a topper. Shirts and ties were easily chosen as they both favoured the same classic but dashing style. It was a tiring day, but great fun too.

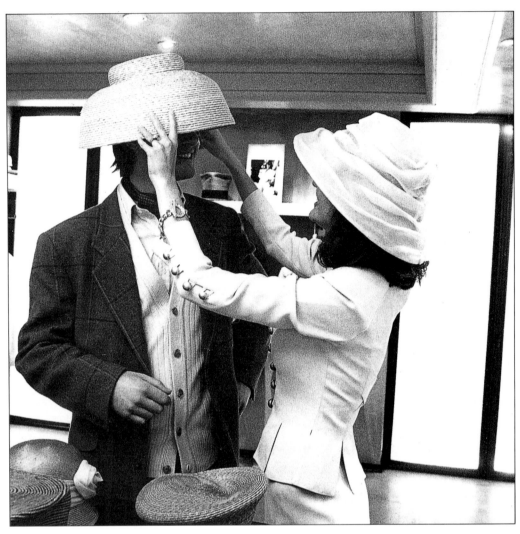

JOSEPH

ANNOUNCEMENTS

Keeping an engagement secret is difficult. One of the symptoms of the condition is an urgent desire to tell the world your wonderful news so that everyone can share in your joy. But a little restraint is necessary, initially at any rate. Unless you are completely estranged from them, your parents should be the first people to be told. If your fiancé has asked your father whether he may marry you, your parents obviously know. Your fiancé's parents should be informed as soon as possible, ideally in person by you both to give them the opportunity to congratulate you and celebrate together. Very often the news is no surprise but the reality of the announcement will be a thrill.

Next you should consider relatives and friends, especially elderly ones who might be hurt to hear the news second-hand. They can be informed at once by telephone or in a handwritten note. Close friends can be told next. Anyone else can hear by word of mouth or through the newspapers. There is no need to inform work colleagues if you don't want to – some girls feel it is none of their business and personalises professional relationships.

The newspapers' court or gazette pages provide a convenient way of informing family and friends scattered over the country that you are engaged to be married and to whom you are engaged. Check charges first. The announcement you wish to be printed should be sent in writing to the paper well in advance of the day you wish it to appear. To avoid embarrassing and irritating mistakes the letter should be typed or printed, should include the date of publication (or state 'to appear as soon as possible') and mention the name of the person to whom the bill should be sent, with their address. An alternative is to telephone the announcement through but do get the person to whom you speak to read it back to you, spelling out every name – even familiar ones such at Matthew or Jane can be misspelt. The bride's parents usually arrange and pay for announcements which generally go into the national broadsheet newspapers, and sometimes a local or county paper in addition. A standard announcement could look like this:

Mr J. G. A. Anderson and Miss M. A. Post

The engagement is announced between James Graham Anthony, eldest son of Professor and Mrs Malcolm Anderson of the Old Barn House, Whitby Newton, Gloucestershire, and Miranda Anne, only daughter of Mrs Gabriel Smith of 123 St Andrew's Square, London SW10 and the late Mr George Post.

The parents' names are included to make it clear exactly which James Anderson and Miranda Post are involved – there may well be more than one. It is a matter of preference whether you list all your Christian names and whether addresses are included, in full or at all. A short, informal announcement could simply give the following details:

Mr P. L. Grinling and Miss C. R. Bilton

Patrick Grinling and Caroline Bilton wish to announce that they are engaged to be married.

In the case of an army officer's engagement, his or her regiment is often included after the Christian names. If you and your partner have been living together for some time, you may prefer to announce that you are getting married, rather than that you are engaged, shortly before the day. If the marriage is to be very quiet or abroad you can include this information, with an indication of the date and place ('quietly next Spring', 'in Rome on August 15th'), from which friends will understand that they should not automatically expect an invitation to the wedding.

A broken engagement is a sad event, and the formalities should be completed as quickly as possible. These depend on the stage in your engagement at which the break occurs. An announcement in the papers before invitations have been sent out can be worded:

Mr G. Acre and Miss H. Sands

The marriage arranged between Mr George Acre and Miss Harriet Sands will not take place.

Your letter to the papers should be signed both by you and by your fiancé. If the invitations have been sent, all guests should be informed in writing (printed, typed or handwritten) that the event has been cancelled. If there is not time to write then all guests should be telephoned. This may be an occasion when you would prefer to enlist the help of close family to make the phone calls. It isn't necessary to go into details or say why the engagement has been broken.

INTRODUCTIONS

Once they hear that you are engaged to be married, everyone you know will want to meet your fiancé and everyone he knows will want to meet you. One way of making these introductions is to give an engagement party. This can be entirely informal and no guest should feel he has to bring a present, although many do. It is quite likely that such a party cannot accommodate everyone you know so you should also be prepared to do the social rounds, accepting invitations to drinks and dinner whenever possible. Don't exhaust yourselves, however, and consult each other before you accept any invitation. If you don't, you may find yourselves getting into a terrible tangle of double-bookings from which it will be troublesome and embarrassing to extricate yourselves.

In addition, either or both sets of parents may wish to give a drinks party to introduce their child's future husband/wife to their friends. If the bride is moving away from her previous home to a place where her new husband's family is established, his parents should certainly give such a party, either before the wedding or afterwards when she has arrived in the area. As well as their relations and friends they might like to invite friends' children with whom they think their new daughter-in-law might have something in common, and perhaps any of their son's close friends whom she has not yet met.

STAGE 1 CHECKLIST

Starting soon after you become engaged

◇ Announce engagement

◇ Choose engagement ring

◇ Research possible dates with families, minister, etc.

◇ Decide date and confirm with minister and families

◇ Read text of service

◇ In Scotland and for civil weddings: take documents to registrar

◇ Arrange calling of Banns

◇ Work out budget with parents

◇ Decide time of wedding, number of guests, format, etc.

◇ Decide style of wedding (flowers, food, drink, etc.)

◇ Book reception location and caterers

◇ Order invitations

◇ Plan wedding cake

◇ Choose and book photographer and video company

◇ Book hire cars and other vehicles

◇ Ask bridesmaids, best man

◇ Choose your and your bridesmaids' dresses and shoes

◇ Compile wedding gift lists

◇ Consult minister and organist to decide service order and music

◇ Make appointments to see doctor, dentist, lawyer

◇ Compile local hotel information

THE BRIDE'S PARENTS

The role of the bride's mother has changed radically in the space of a generation, while the bride's father's role has changed hardly at all. Our mothers' weddings were quite likely to have been masterminded entirely by **their** mothers but, today, a bride expects the organisation of her wedding to be either a joint effort or entirely her own responsibility. The bride's father, meanwhile, is still not expected to do much more than guide his daughter up the aisle, give her away, and pay some or all of the bills after the event. Many fathers do much more, of course (see below), but if he is detached from the intimate details of the advance organisation your father may be an invaluable roving troubleshooter on the day of the wedding, producing lunch for the bride before an afternoon ceremony, dealing calmly with telephone calls and coping with any minor problems which may arise.

You and your parents (if they are helping with the organisation) need to sit down together soon after you have become engaged and have a practical discussion. You don't have to decide at this stage exactly how you want everything to be – better not, in fact, as your parents may have some excellent suggestions. You, your mother and father should explain anything you feel strongly about, such as the location of the marriage ceremony, the format of invitations or the preference of one florist over another. With any luck there won't be any clashes of interest and everyone's wishes can be accommodated. If there are conflicts, negotiate and sort them out as soon as possible. Don't be forced into having the type of wedding your parents would like you to have if it is genuinely not what you want but be prepared to compromise graciously on points you don't feel too strongly about. Money needs to be discussed early on as it will probably influence the size and the type of wedding you have.

Once these general matters have been dealt with, take a look at the Stage One, Two and Three checklists on pages 25, 33, 43 and 47, and allocate clear areas of responsibility. If the bridesmaids' dresses are being made in the city where you live and work, and the reception and caterers are near your parents, it becomes obvious who should organise which. This doesn't mean you won't be involved with each other's tasks. On the contrary, communication is the key to organising any event successfully. Frequent consultation will ensure that everyone knows what is going on and can contribute ideas and suggestions, while preventing confusion and argument.

The bride's mother's responsibilities traditionally include everything to do with the guest list, including the sending of invitations, after consultation with you, your future husband and his parents, and the recording of acceptances. She can also act as a channel for informal information, answering enquiries about your gift lists and, on a more personal level, liaising with the groom's mother about clothes so that their colours and styles don't clash on the day (your mother's choice takes precedence). Finally, to ensure she isn't stranded while you and your father travel to the church together on the wedding day, she could ask a male friend or relative who is coming to the wedding to drive her and escort her to her pew. This isn't necessary if there is room for her to travel in the car with the bridesmaids and an usher is briefed to take her to her seat.

MOTHER

'If I'd known beforehand about the sore feet tramping across London in search of the perfect wedding dress and the nervous strain of trying to curb a guest list that was beginning to offer strong competition to a royal garden party, would I still have gone through with it? Of course I would. Lucy and Brooks announced their engagement on Good Friday and he asked my husband if he had any objection to his marrying our daughter. What objection could there be? He was good-natured, good-mannered and in love. Whilst Lucy booked interviews for the two of them with Father Stephen Louden and Rabbi Friedlander, each of whom pointed out their duties to themselves, each other and their God, I concentrated on the equally fundamental problem of what I was going to wear. Eventually I chose a riot of printed silk topped by a large straw hat, enough to banish any nervousness on the day. When the time came, everything went like clockwork. All the nagging worries of the past months – doubts about the weather, the small misprints on the service sheets, the size of the tents for the evening barbecue – fell sharply into perspective as I watched Lucy and Brooks exchange their vows, for whom this meant the beginning of a new life.'

FATHER

'It's not only women who worry about clothes for weddings. I have a morning coat, made in 1935 and inherited from my father. But there were also Lucy's two large brothers to kit out, not only with suits. Where are your black shoes? When did you last see your cufflinks? Twenty years of bringing up a family persuades me it is chiefly a training in lost property. The wedding was at the Royal Military Academy where I had worked for twenty-five years and knew exactly who did what. The Chaplain's secretary books the chapel and Chaplain. The Chaplain arranges the order of service and rehearsals. The Verger arranges the chapel and the organist the music. Neville, the chef, decided the menu and organised the cake and the Mess Secretary the champagne. I thought I'd done my stuff. But I'd forgotten security considerations, and signposts to guide the guests. These were sorted out and, suddenly, there was no more time to forsee disasters. The sun shone. The trumpeter played as if at the Royal Tournament. The newly-married couple drove away in a vintage Lagonda – I just snatched a kiss from my darling daughter. No regrets – the pang I'd felt when Brooks had come to tell us of their engagement was a thing of the past. We had acquired a delightful son-in-law. My wife was radiant. And the boys had looked as tidy as anyone could wish.'

THE GROOM'S PARENTS

As far as the organisation of your wedding goes, your fiancé's parents in their traditional roles are not involved at all, beyond providing your mother with a list of their guests, promptly and with all the correct titles and addresses. Even if his parents make a tactful offer of financial help which is accepted, they should not expect to take over the organisation of any aspect of the wedding unless specifically asked. Help offered and accepted could be in kind rather than financial. A florist mother or wine-merchant father of the groom should keep in close touch with you and your parents.

Although the groom's mother doesn't have an official role, she plays an important part in the run-up to her son's wedding and on his wedding day, starting with the announcement of your engagement. Unless they are already friends, she writes to your parents saying how happy she and your fiancé's father are about the engagement and inviting your parents for an informal drink or to tea. If they live far apart, she should try to arrange a meeting at a place of mutual convenience or invite them to stay for a weekend. If they don't contact your parents, it will probably be better in the long run if your parents cast etiquette aside and make the first move. Everything will run smoothly on the wedding day if they have previously met but, if it really is not possible, photographs could be exchanged instead.

Your future mother-in-law, if she has any sense, will try to get to know you as her son's future wife and make friends. As a special gesture of friendship she may offer you a personal present such as a piece of family jewellery, which you should accept and, if possible, wear on your wedding day with your wedding dress or going-away outfit. She should discuss what you would like to call her. Her Christian name or the name by which she is known to her family is least pretentious and most sensible. If she doesn't bring up the subject you can, or you can simply address her by her Christian name after the wedding or just before, perhaps following a buffer period of studiously calling her nothing.

If your future in-laws live a long way from the location of the wedding they may have to stay somewhere overnight and should organise this for themselves as far in advance as possible. Your parents could offer to arrange for them to stay with friends, and should certainly supply them with information and recommendations about local hotels. On the wedding day, they should be in church a good quarter of an hour before the service, and if there is a receiving line at the reception they will stand between your parents and you. They sit at the top table and if there is dancing your father should ask your new mother-in-law to dance (and her husband your mother) soon after you have taken to the floor.

IN-LAWS

The importance of your relationship with your future husband's parents cannot be overestimated but it is unlikely that the perfect relationship will fall into your lap. You will almost certainly have to work at it. If you get it right, or anywhere near right, you will be glad that you made the effort and will reap great rewards. Then, even if you never get it right in spite of hard work, you'll know it's not your fault. Above all, it is vital that if anyone loses their temper or behaves badly, it isn't you. It may not be obvious at the time but later on you will be glad that you didn't force a confrontation.

Useful tools in forging a good relationship are imagination, humility, relaxed self-confidence and a dose of amateur analysis. Take a step back and look at the sort of person you are, the sort they are, and be realistic. Remember that they may find you threatening, even if they don't recognise the fact. Who is this independent, self-controlled and poised young woman with whom their son has fallen in love? Does she expect to take him over just like that after he's spent a lifetime being, first and foremost, their son? Your in-laws will be suffering anxieties and insecurities as well as, astonishingly, a natural desire to be liked. You can appear just as daunting to them as they do to you.

Consider your fiancé's relationship with his family. Is his father a patriarchal type who likes to be the focus of the family and resents the distraction you present? Does your fiancé live at home with his parents, in which case they may initially find your frequent presence a challenge to their 'authority', especially if you stay overnight with him?

Even if such obstacles are present, you can still establish a perfectly workable and enjoyable relationship with your in-laws. Let it develop naturally, based on honesty. Talk openly to them about things that genuinely interest you. Be helpful at meal-times. Give them a chance to like you for what you are, not for what you think they want you to be. Remember you are stuck with them for life. Let them see that you genuinely care about their son and want him to be happy and fulfilled in life, but that you aren't hanging around his neck. Treat them as you would new colleagues at work, developing a professional working relationship as the most important people (until now) in your fiancé's life. You may well find it develops into genuine friendship.

GOLDEN RULES

DO

▶ Be open and relaxed
▶ Remember that they are your fiancé's parents and have known him all his life
▶ Try to develop a relationship based on honesty and respect
▶ Let them know you are secure in your role
▶ Learn from them about your fiancé, his character, background and childhood
▶ Listen to what they say
▶ Be on time when they are expecting you
▶ Give them a good idea of your family and background
▶ Ask about their interests and experiences
▶ Tell them about your activities outside the home
▶ Try to answer their questions about your attitude to your forthcoming marriage (within reason)
▶ Consider having one of their daughters or other young relation as a bridesmaid
▶ Be tactful about your intention to continue your career after having children (if this is the case)
▶ Compliment her on her hat on your wedding day, if you possibly can

DON'T

▶ Be icily reserved (even if this is your natural reaction from shyness)
▶ Forget that your youth may threaten your fiancé's mother
▶ Assume automatic friendship or be over-familiar
▶ Show off
▶ Alter your opinions to suit theirs
▶ Allow yourself to be bullied
▶ Let them foist their daughters on you as bridesmaids
▶ Call round without prior warning
▶ Yawn when family reminiscences are trotted out
▶ Be too offhand about the role of the housewife
▶ Pretend you will give up work after having children if you don't intend to
▶ Insist on excluding them from celebrations at Christmas or on your husband's birthday
▶ Speak when it's better to say nothing
▶ Let them put you off marrying their son
▶ Ignore them on your wedding day

2
PRACTICAL MATTERS

FINANCE AND BUDGETING

Getting married, in a place of worship or at a register office, is not exorbitantly expensive. It's the trappings – the dress, attendants, flowers, celebrations – which are expensive. It is tiresome, but absolutely necessary, that you pay attention to money early in the preparations for your wedding – before those preparations really begin, in fact. It is very easy to overspend. Costs mount up quickly and it would be a shame to spoil your wedding with money worries because you didn't calculate realistically from the start. The first matter to consider is who will pay for what.

The groom's expenses traditionally include rings, all fees connected with the marriage ceremony itself (but not embellishments such as church flower decorations and music during the service), flowers for bride and bridesmaids and buttonholes for himself and any other of the men, gifts for the attendants, and the honeymoon. The rest (the major part) of the costs traditionally fall to the bride's father. Today these simple rules can apply, if you want them to, but more often than not they are broken. You and your fiancé may earn more than your parents, and your future in-laws may wish to contribute.

Money has always been a subject which causes embarrassment, especially at a time like this when romance and tradition are supposed to be the order of the day. You must overcome all such inhibitions and talk openly about money with your parents, finding out what they (and you) can afford. If you are organising your wedding but your parents are paying, it is vital to discuss an overall sum with them. They may not realise what things cost, however, so you could begin this discussion armed with some examples and estimates.

Offers of financial assistance can cause hurt feelings and rifts unless made, and accepted or rejected, with the utmost tact. If your fiancé's parents don't know your parents well and make a direct offer of help, your parents might feel it a matter of honour to refuse. Instead, your fiancé could mention to you that his parents would like to pay for the champagne, or the flowers in church and at the reception, and you could convey this to your parents at the right moment. Alternatively, if you have been told that your in-laws-to-be or your fiancé would like to help, you could ask your mother (or whichever parent is less likely to stand on their pride) to suggest an expense where help would be welcome.

Although it can cause embarrassment

and misunderstandings, money can also help solve family difficulties. If your parents are divorced and one of them is acting as host at your wedding together with their spouse, your other parent may feel left out. He or she could be involved by making a specific financial contribution, for example, towards the cost of your dress.

Once it has been decided who will pay for what, and once the estimates have come in to give you and your parents an idea of what you and they can afford, they may prefer you not to know exactly how much everything costs. If you can resist the urge to know, don't press them for details.

BUDGETING

The list on page 36 may look daunting at first glance, and you might have to tone down some of your wilder ideas because of what they would cost. However, there are plenty of ways of keeping costs down and allocating funds for maximum effect. Even if your ideas and budget are compatible, you will want to be sure you are getting value for money. Techniques to help you budget efficiently include:

▶ Research and planning
▶ Prioritising
▶ DIY and borrowing
▶ Realism and record-keeping

Research and planning

The first consideration is a calculation of the total sum available to you to spend on your wedding, from whatever source or sources. After this, the next most significant requirement for your research and planning is time. The more of it you have, the better your research and planning can be. This is especially true for summer weddings, for which the best professionals and most popular locations are booked up early. Six months' notice is usually sufficient. Make your own checklist based on the one suggested. Apply to various caterers, florists, etc. (ones whose work you have seen or can arrange to see, or have already experienced at other people's weddings) for their literature with cost guidelines. Follow this with a request for estimates for your own exact requirements. Examine estimates carefully for 'hidden' charges like the cost of providing lunch for the staff who will be serving your meal. Estimates from three different firms will give you an idea of competitive prices. If you know exactly whom you want to do certain things – the cake for example – you could perhaps ask them for price guides for two or three different specifications.

Prioritising

This involves deciding which things you feel strongly about, the lack of which will diminish your wedding day for you, and which things you really don't mind about. You may have set your heart on a pony and trap, for example, but be perfectly happy with the local church choir instead of professional singers. Sometimes priorities are set by family or local custom. In the north of England, for example, it is generally considered inhospitable to give your wedding guest anything less than a decent meal, and in Scotland the celebrations often

include reeling or a ceilidh, whereas in southern England the ceremony is often followed simply by a stand-up reception with champagne and finger food or canapés. Many families would consider a pay bar the height of meanness and vulgarity, while the idea worries others not at all.

DIY and borrowing

One great charm of doing things yourself, asking friends to do things for you, or borrowing things, is that they can feel more personal to you than anything a professional can provide. If you do ask friends to help, or for loans, always ask tactfully so that they can say no without embarrassment. Don't ask at all if what you want is irreplaceable and breakable, or you are in the least nervous about harm coming to it. Always be prepared for the worst by having insurance and contingency plans. It is surprising what it is possible to borrow. A married friend whose wedding dress was a wild extravagance may be delighted to lend it, since the loan makes her feel better about the cost. Friends with a large house or barn may be happy for you to use the space, so long as you provide extra insurance if necessary and pay for the room to be cleaned by professionals afterwards.

Realism and record-keeping

Be realistic, not romantic, about prices, and set aside a sum for unexpected costs and price rises. Get everything in writing, read the small print, keep every single piece of paper with information, estimates and

---

STAGE 2 CHECKLIST

Starting 2 or 3 months before wedding

◇ Go over Stage 1 Checklist and do anything you have forgotten

◇ Buy wedding ring(s) and send to be engraved

◇ Order service sheets

◇ Ask person to make first toast

◇ Check groom's and best man's clothes arrangements

◇ Write thank-you letters for presents

◇ Organise crèche and/or security arrangements

◇ If taking husband's name, inform bank, tax office, etc. and get forms to have passport changed

◇ Organise going away clothes and honeymoon clothes

◇ Check car parking arrangements at church and reception

◇ Draw up guest list and send invitations enclosing travel and hotel information

◇ Make lists and family trees for group photographs and send to photographer

◇ Go to church to hear banns read

◇ Arrange wedding rehearsal

◇ Make appointments for hair, nails

◇ Rehearse wearing veil

◇ Check progress of wedding cake

◇ Have a night out with girlfriends

calculations on it and make sure it has the correct dates on it (the date of the document as well as the date of the wedding). Start a well-labelled filing system at once, making sure everyone involved in the organisation understands it and uses it. Make notes during telephone calls and file these. Follow any telephone confirmation with a prompt note, if possible delivered by hand so that there can be no doubt about it having arrived. Type or print important letters if there is any chance of your writing being illegible, and keep duplicates whenever possible. When using the post, send things by one of the types of mail which guarantee delivery or provide insurance, or get a date-stamped certificate of posting (the latter costs nothing, just ask for it at the counter when you post the item). Don't assume something has arrived if you don't get confirmation – check by telephone. You will soon get into the habit of keeping everything down to the smallest receipt. Let the spectre of something going wrong on your wedding day urge you to be efficient beforehand.

CUTTING COSTS

If you practice the four techniques above you will be well on the way to making your money go as far as it can, as well as being a paragon of efficiency. If you or a friend or close relation who offers their services has relevant expertise – such as being a designer or dressmaker, organist or singer, florist or superb cook – it is sensible to make the most of this. There are two other ways to economise. One is to make many small cuts; the other is to cut out some major

expense or expenses entirely. A combination of the two is probably least painful.

The dress

One of the greatest expenses, traditionally borne by your parents, is that of your wedding dress. You might like to wear your mother's or sister's wedding dress and veil. If you or a relation or friend is a capable dressmaker, your dress could be home-made either from a wedding dress or ball-gown pattern, or from one made by a professional pattern-cutter to your own design. Another alternative is to hire a dress. There are many reputable clothes-hire companies, some devoted exclusively to wedding clothes, that will alter one of their designer dresses to fit you, and the final cost is a fraction of the price of a new dress. Some of these firms will, by prior arrangement, buy your new dress from you after the event, or you could advertise your dress and sell it that way. Many brides have their wedding dress altered or dyed and thereby justify the cost by getting many years' wear from it.

Bridesmaids and pages

Most of these cost-cutting ideas apply to bridesmaids' dresses too. Another idea is to buy fabric for the dresses and ask the bridesmaids or their parents to make their own or have them made to a pattern supplied by you. If your attendants are bearing some or all of the cost, however, it is only fair to consult them or their parents about fabric and style so they can use the clothes afterwards.

If you or your fiancé is an officer in the armed forces, you may find that your or his regiment has miniature versions of the dress uniform which can be lent to you for pageboys to wear.

Reception

For the reception, a marquee in your garden is usually a major expense, especially with lighting, heating, a dance floor, dais and furniture. There are also considerable inconveniences attached to having crowds of people walking through your home (especially considering the unpredictability of the weather). You may find another location, such as a local church hall, school hall or dining-room, is more suitable and a fraction of the cost. Hotels and clubs vary hugely and may provide what you want at a price you can afford, but you will have to use their caterers, which rules out another possible economy – preparing the food yourself. There are several excellent books on celebration food, which should be planned a long way in advance. It can also be made well in advance (though not too far), but you should practice making, freezing and defrosting small quantities, taking careful note of timing and quality at each stage. If you don't have enough freezer space, you could borrow friends' freezer space or even hire extra freezers. Make sure you have insurance cover for freezers and the food inside them in case of disaster.

If you or your mother bakes cakes, yours could be homemade, and if you baulk at decorating it you can pay someone else to do that for you.

Drinks

Champagne is the traditional drink for a wedding, but a fine dry sparkling wine is more pleasant than a raw, cheap champagne and can be considerably less expensive. If you are not yourself interested in wine you could commission a responsible member of your family who is, and who understands it, to research different types and prices with a reputable wine merchant. Keep tabs on their research, however, and make it clear exactly who has the last word and who makes the booking or places the order and confirms it.

Buying all drinks on a sale-or-return basis is sensible. If non-alcoholic drinks were more interesting and more readily available at weddings, many more people would drink them for a large part or all of the day's celebrations. Cold, freshly squeezed fruit juice or a fruit cocktail (with lots of fruit in it, served in generous-sized glasses) is more refreshing than alcohol on a hot summer's day, and cheaper to provide. So is a really delicious Earl Grey or other fine tea, in any weather. Children and guests who are driving should have something delicious to drink, even if it's only one of the many carbonated mineral waters now available. This or jugs of iced water with slices of lemon in it should be placed on every table, along with the wine, at a sit-down meal.

Transport

There is absolutely no reason why you have to have a hired car to take you to church, so long as there is a reliable family

car which is large enough to accommodate your dress without crushing it. Make sure that the car is serviced, is immaculately clean inside and out, and that its petrol and windscreen-washing fluid tanks are full. Have a back-up car organised too, just in case. You will probably want two cars anyway, one for the bridesmaids.

When you and your husband leave for your honeymoon after the celebrations, the simplest and cheapest method of transport is your or his car. If you are in London, Edinburgh or another city with traditional shiny black cabs, you could go away in great style in one of these (brief the company or driver first so it is spotlessly clean). A motorbike or pedal bike, especially if it's a tandem, are unusual methods of going-away transport which are picturesque and inexpensive, but your clothes should take account of the practicalities of riding astride. If someone you know has an antique

or unusual vehicle, or another form of transport such as a pony and trap or even an aeroplane, you could ask if they would allow you to leave for your honeymoon in that, as a wedding present. But do ask quietly and tactfully, so that they can refuse without embarrassment, and be prepared to pay maintenance costs at the very least.

Stationery, flowers and photographs

Anything you can make yourself or get friends to do will help cut costs, and be more personal. Handmade invitations or service sheets are a possibility. They should be written with enormous care to ensure that the handwriting is legible, and can be photocopied on coloured or white card or paper. Your service sheet could be constructed from photocopied handwritten pages tied together with a ribbon.

Flower arranging takes much longer than you may realise and you will probably not have time to do it yourself. A friend may, but make sure you are satisfied that their skill and style are up to the job. The answer may be to keep the flowers extremely simple. In summer, it may be possible to use flowers from your own, your parents' and friends' gardens, but these will almost certainly have to be supplemented with bought flowers. Find out by asking around or looking in the Yellow Pages where your local wholesale flower market is, and what hours it operates. Many flower markets are open to individuals as well as florists, so long as you buy in quantity. You will need plenty of flowers to make an impact both in church and at the reception.

Economising on photographs is risky. If you don't employ a reliable professional photographer you may end up without a record of your wedding. Consider finding a photographer who doesn't charge an attendance fee, and beware of paying for an album containing a few prints when the same money would buy more photographs without the album. If money is a real problem, and you have a friend whom you know is a good amateur photographer and would be willing, you could give her or him a dozen rolls of film, colour and/or black-and-white, and ask them to take the lot and hand back the films for you to have processed and printed. As with a professional, you would need to brief him or her about formal group shots.

Insurance

Most weddings go ahead as planned, and the premium for insuring your wedding is therefore tiny. It is sensible to insure, for your peace of mind as much as anything. As with any insurance policy, check exactly under what circumstances you can claim, and what is covered.

What does a wedding cost?

People often ask 'how much does a wedding cost?' The answer is as much or as little as you want and varies according to whether you use local suppliers or large city-based firms. The rule of thumb is that everything costs more than you expect it to but some research along the lines of the following Checklist of Costs will give you a guide to the cost of your ideal wedding.

CHECKLIST OF COSTS

The following is a general checklist to help you research prices

ANNOUNCEMENTS
Engagement: national papers
Engagement: local papers
Wedding announcements

STATIONERY
Invitations and envelopes
Postage
Service sheets
Any other

CEREMONY
Banns and other documentation
Transport to and from ceremony
Officiant
Organist and choir
Childminder or crèche organiser
Any other

CLOTHES
Wedding dress and veil
Shoes, underwear and accessories
Going-away outfit, hat and shoes
Bridesmaids' and page's clothes
Their shoes and accessories
Groom's clothes and shoes
Any other

PERSONAL
Hair and make-up
Flowers for mothers
Gifts for attendants
Tips
Any other

FLOWERS
At church/place of worship
Bride's bouquet and head-dress
Bridesmaids' posies and head-dresses
Men's buttonholes
At reception
Any other

PHOTOGRAPHY/VIDEO
Engagement photographs
Photographer's attendance fee
Prints or album of photographs
Video
Additional copies of video
Sound recording in church
Any other

RECEPTION
Location: hotel, marquee, hall or house
Lighting and heating
Champagne or sparkling wine
Other alcoholic drinks
Soft drinks
Food – canapés followed by a full meal
Food – finger food for stand-up reception
Cake
Hire of equipment such as linen, china, cutlery, table decorations, furniture, microphone
Staff
Music
Other entertainment such as magician, fireworks
Any other

HONEYMOON
Passport in bride's new name
Visas and vaccinations
Going-away vehicle
Hotel for first night
Travel
Holiday
Spending money
Special clothes
Any other

THE DATE

The main considerations in setting a date for your wedding are the length of your engagement and the season in which you want to be married. There may also be family considerations; you or your fiancé may have relations coming from abroad who need time to make their travel arrangements. It may be that you or your fiancé will be starting a new job or taking a posting abroad and need to arrange your wedding speedily. Practical matters can also influence the date: the church or the place where you would like the reception to be held after the ceremony may already be booked on certain dates.

In general, however, around six months is a good length for an engagement. You both have time to adjust to the prospect of being married, and time to organise the wedding without being hurried.

Too long an engagement can become a strain when you want to get on with your life as a married couple and not wait interminably for the event.

The traditional season for weddings is summer. Winter is least popular, although weddings around the time of Christmas and New Year are often especially memorable. In terms of style, a winter wedding with holly and Christmas trees, bridesmaids dressed in red velvet or tartan, and candles lighting up the darkness can be just as beautiful as a floral summer wedding. If your parents have a lovely garden where you want to hold the reception, summer is better for you, but this particular circumstance only applies to a small proportion of people. Flowers are available throughout the year, flown in to flower markets from abroad, so there is very little constraint on the date in this respect.

There is no need to be married on a Saturday. It is a relatively recent development that Saturday has been adopted as the automatic day for a wedding. This has happened in part because it is increasingly likely that the bride as well as the groom has a demanding job which occupies her weekdays. One reason for being married on another day is that many package holidays begin on Saturday, so if your honeymoon is to be spent abroad you may consider being married on the preceding Thursday or Friday. If you marry on a weekday, guests who work will have to take time off to come and may not be able to come at all but this is not such a problem if you plan an intimate wedding with just a handful of family and friends. Register offices tend to be more heavily booked on Saturdays than weekdays, so you could possibly be married during the week and have a service of blessing and the reception on the Saturday. Such an arrangement is not always possible so consult your minister to avoid disappointment (see page 82 for detailed information on Services of Blessing).

Weddings are rarely held on Sundays in the Church of England and other Christian churches because it is the busiest day in the week for both church and minister. If you do want to be married on a Sunday, ask with utmost tact and make it clear you realise you are asking a favour. Back up your request with some good reasons for it. When a church is popular and all Saturdays are booked up for the summer, or in special circumstances like the quiet marriage of a widow or widower, a minister will sometimes consider conducting a Sunday wedding. He may also be more sympathetic to the request if you are known to him as a regular member of his congregation. The Jewish sabbath begins at sundown on Friday and ends at sundown on Saturday, so Jewish weddings are held on Sundays rather than Saturdays.

Religious festivals and seasons may be significant as the church may be needed for special events or weddings may not be allowed at all. But otherwise it is really a matter of taste at what time of year you finally decide to be married. Any date will do, as long as everyone is happy, including the person who will marry you, both sets of parents, and any professionals such as caterers and musicians on whom you have set your heart.

The date of your marriage should be agreeable to the minister, whom you must consult before making a decision, and to both families.

THE PLACE

Most people choose to be married in a place of worship because they feel that the service and surroundings suitably reflect the seriousness of what they are undertaking as well as giving voice to the joy of the occasion. Most religions, denominations and ministers welcome couples who want to have a religious ceremony, once they are satisfied that they want it for the right reasons. Some officiants are stricter than others about matters like attending church beforehand and if you are planning a Roman Catholic wedding you will generally have to attend instruction groups on the meaning of marriage as well as attending church services.

Most ministers take the view that this is an opportunity for them to start a marriage off on the right note and they are therefore more than happy to welcome the couple into their church, regardless of whether or not they have seen them there before their engagement. The general rule in Christian churches is that you or your fiancé has to have been baptised, but if neither of you qualifies in this respect it is doubtful whether you would be refused Christian marriage on this account alone.

Once you have decided upon a religious marriage service, the question is where to hold it. The laws governing places where you can be married vary with Jewish and Quaker weddings and are different in Scotland. For everyone else, your parish church or regular place of worship is the obvious answer, but you might prefer to be married from your parents' home in their parish church. In this case you may have to qualify to be married there in one of several ways. In the Church of England these include a residential qualification (for which you would have to move to your parents' home for a certain time), joining the electoral roll of the church if you are not already on it, or getting a Special Licence to marry there. You should consult the minister about these different methods, asking him to explain them to you in detail, and in consultation with him choose the one most appropriate to your needs. For additional information contact your diocesan office.

The alternative to a religious marriage service is a purely civil marriage in your local register office or in another licensed building (if proposed new laws are enacted) such as a hotel or stately home. Ask at your register office for details of the current situation and the names of possible places near you. For a civil marriage, and for a religious marriage outside the Church of England, various civil preliminaries must be completed (see pages 46-47). Contact your local register office to establish exactly what these are and what documents (such as your birth certificate or other proofs of identity and current marital status) you will need to produce. The civil preliminaries cannot begin more than three months before the date of the wedding, and you cannot book your wedding date until the preliminaries are underway. The exact length of this period is presently under review but will be either three or six months – check with your local office. After this period your official 'permission' to marry expires and you need to start the preliminaries all over again.

In a few denominations and religions it is necessary to have a civil marriage in addition to the religious ceremony. This can occur where the place of worship or the officiant is not licensed for marriage. Check with your minister if you are in doubt about this. Another circumstance in which you might choose a register-office wedding is if you and your fiancé are of different religions. A civil marriage followed by blessings bestowed by one or both religions can sometimes satisfy both families and avoid acrimony arising from a need to choose between them.

A civil marriage can be followed by a religious service of blessing or other dignified ceremony which will give more satisfying expression to the depth of your feelings and the significance of the occasion (see page 82).

Your local parish church or your parents' parish church is the usual location for a Christian marriage service. If you are faced with a choice, ask yourself where you feel you belong as you will want to be married in a building which is rich in meaning for you.

THE TIME

	11.00am WEDDING		12 noon WEDDING	
	Sit-down luncheon		*Buffet luncheon*	
	Dance in evening after local dinner parties		*Dancing*	
10am	**10.15** Ushers at church **10.30** Groom and best man in their seats **10.45** Groom's parents in	their seats: organist begins **10.55** Bridesmaids arrive Bride's mother escorted to her seat		
11am	**11.00** Bride arrives Photographs at church door **11.50** Church service finishes Photographs at church door		**11.15** Ushers at church **11.30** Groom and best man in their seats **11.45** Groom's parents in	their seats: organist begins **11.55** Bridesmaids arrive, bride's mother escorted to her seat
12pm	**12.15** Arrive at reception Photographs Guests meanwhile served with champagne and soft drinks	**12.30** Bride and groom join reception party and line up with both sets of parents to receive guests	**12.00** Bride arrives Photographs at church door **12.50** Church service finishes Photographs at church door	
1pm	**1.30** Best man asks for silence and announces lunch Anyone who hasn't already done so sits down according	to formal seating plan displayed at entrance First course is served	**1.15** Arrive at reception Photographs Champagne and soft drinks served to guests	**1.30** No formal receiving line, but bride and groom stay in one place together
2pm	**2.00** Best man, bride and groom go to dais Bride and groom cut cake Speeches	**2.30** Speeches finish Rest of lunch is served, including wedding cake	**2.00** Lunch is announced, guests are served from buffet Bride and groom continue to greet guests	**2.45** Best man, bride and groom go to dais Bride and groom cut cake Speeches
3pm	**3.45** Bride and groom go to change		**3.10** Speeches end Wedding cake, tea and coffee served	**3.15** Band begins playing Bride and groom circulate amongst guests and dance
4pm	**4.00** Bride and groom 'go away', to return later for the dance; they may change clothes	**4.30** Guests have dispersed to their homes, to hotels and to house parties previously arranged by the bride	**4.30** Bride and groom go to change	
5pm			**5.00** Bride and groom leave for their honeymoon Band resumes playing	
6pm				
7pm	**7.00** Dinner parties at local private houses, previously arranged by the bride		**7.00** Band stops playing Guests gradually say their farewells and leave	
8pm				
9pm	**9.00** Guests begin to arrive Dancing starts, with bride and groom taking the lead			
10pm	**10.00** Firework display outdoors At some point between now and the end of dancing at	2.00am, the bride and groom slip away quietly to their first-night hotel		

THE TIME

2.30pm WEDDING		4.00pm WEDDING		
Stand-up reception		*Sit-down supper* *Dancing*		
				10am
				11am
12.30 Ushers, groom and best man meet for lunch and instructions				12pm
1.45 Ushers at church				1pm
2.00 Groom and best man in their seats 2.15 Groom's parents in their seats: organist begins	2.25 Bridesmaids arrive, bride's mother escorted to seat 2.30 Bride arrives Photographs at church door	2.00 Ushers, groom and best man meet for lunch and instructions		2pm
3.20 Church service finishes Photographs at church door 3.45 Arrive at reception Photographs	Guests served with champagne, soft drinks and plenty of finger food	3.15 Ushers at church 3.30 Groom and best man in their seats 3.45 Groom's parents in their	seats: organist begins 3.55 Bridesmaids arrive Bride's mother escorted to her seat	3pm
4.00 Bride and groom join guests and circulate		4.00 Bride arrives Photographs at church door 4.50 Church service finishes Photographs at church door		4pm
5.30 Best man, bride and groom, go to dais Bride and groom cut wedding cake	Short speeches, because everyone is standing up 5.45 Speeches end Cake, tea and coffee served	5.15 Arrive at reception Photographs Champagne and soft drinks served, together with canapés	5.30 Bride and groom stand together near dais to greet guests	5pm
6.15 Bride and groom go to change	6.45 Bride and groom go away on honeymoon Guests leave	6.30 Best man announces cutting of cake Guests who have not already sat down do so according to	formal seating plan Bride and groom cut wedding cake Speeches	6pm
		7.00 Speeches end Supper is served		7pm
		8.00 Band starts to play Bride and groom circulate and dance		8pm
		9.30 Bride and groom go to change		9pm
		10.00 Bride and groom leave on honeymoon Band resumes playing and continues until midnight or	until last guests leave, whichever is sooner	10pm

The time at which you decide the actual ceremony should take place is tied up with the types of celebration you want to follow it. This chart shows examples of four weddings, each at a different time, with four combinations of reception or other party afterwards.

CHOICES

Every aspect of the organisation of a wedding involves making choices. If you were indecisive before, you might find you are cured of it by the time you reach the altar. Pen and paper are wonderful aids in the business of making decisions. If you have difficulty deciding, simply list the alternatives, their practical pros and cons and your feelings about them. Go away and do something else before coming back to the list, and you may well find the best choice springs out at you.

THE DRESS

The most personal choice you will have to make concerns your wedding dress.

There are points in favour of all the different sources of dresses. If you buy a dress, you can see the finished effect from the start. Buying may not be the best answer for you if you have a very clear idea of what you want your dress to look like and can't find it on the rails. If you have a very large or long figure or are very small you might find the choice is more limited. And the cost of a designer dress can seem prohibitive. This can be allayed if you sell the dress afterwards or have it altered or dyed so that you can wear it to parties for years to come. The bridal chain-stores offer some dresses that are a great deal less expensive, but make sure you like the fabric as well as the style.

Hiring appeals to many brides because it provides an economically viable way of having the dress of their dreams, with the same advantage as buying in that you can try on various dresses before choosing. Some shops will arrange to buy your dress after your wedding, in order to hire it out to other brides, but you should research this and come to an agreement before the event if possible, not afterwards.

If you make your dress or have it made you need to feel confident that the finished product will be what you want, and that the person making it is skilled. The great thing about a dress made specially for you is that it is uniquely yours. It can be made to any style you like, in any fabric you like. Professional pattern-cutters who will make a pattern to your own design advertise in magazines and newspaper sections devoted to weddings. The end result is quite likely to cost much less than a designer gown. Designer's are professionals, however, and you are probably not, so beware of anything too outrageous, and take your dressmaker's advice about what will suit your figure.

YOUR ATTENDANTS

One of the early decisions you will have to make concerns attendants: how many, of which sex, of what age, and who should they be? You need to ask them and/or their parents well in advance of your wedding because there may be major logistical problems in getting their clothes bought and fitted or made, especially if there are any number of them and they live in different places.

Don't let anyone tell you who your attendants should be. It would be thoughtful of you to include at least one relation or connection of your future husband, but don't let any of your or his relations, or your fiancé himself, make you feel guilty about not choosing anyone in particular.

On the other hand, your choice of attendants offers a wonderful opportunity to build bridges – between two parts of the family which have not been getting on, for example, or by involving your future step-children in your wedding. Your male attendants should be young – not older than fourteen or so – but female attendants can be any age. If any of them are still living at home and dependent on their parents (probably still at school or under 18), it is courteous to ask their parents as well as them if the child may be an attendant, as it is the parents rather than they themselves who will probably do the organising as well as bearing any financial burden.

Every attendant, of whatever age, should be asked in such a way that they can gracefully refuse. A friend who is a contemporary, for instance, may prefer to fulfil the role of the bride's best friend, helping you get dressed on the day and being treated as an honoured guest. She may feel she has grown out of the business of wearing a pretty dress and carrying flowers in the procession. When you ask, you should also make it clear what is involved in the way of expenses, travel and responsibilities on the day. You could also, if it is possible, give them some idea of what they will be wearing – older children can be very touchy on this point and it might be better for them to refuse now than create difficulties later.

If your bridesmaids are to be small children, be prepared for a certain amount of chaos and possibly noise in the aisle on the day. A nervous child may even refuse to go up the aisle when the time comes. You also need to take into account your overall policy on children in church.

BEST MAN

The choice of best man is your fiancé's, but you can encourage him to choose someone whom you believe suitable. A person who tends to drink too much would clearly not make a good choice, however close a friend he is. It is perfectly acceptable for the best man to be a 'best girl', although special tact is involved in the choice. A sister or business partner who is also a good friend of the groom is acceptable, but it would be tactless of him to ask an ex-girlfriend and such a choice would not bode well for your forthcoming marriage. A male friend who is ideal but would prefer not to make the usual speech could fulfil all the other best man's duties, if another friend or relation of the groom is happy and willing to make the speech in his place. You could think of the two men as 'groomsmen' or 'supporters' rather than best men and they could both stand with your fiancé at the steps of the chancel.

USHERS

Ushers play a vital role at a wedding taking place at a church or other place of worship. They welcome guests to the church and the wedding, handing out service sheets, answering the usual queries about which is the bride's and which the groom's side of the church and any other seating arrangements with which guests may not be familiar, and they escort guests to their seats. They ensure that guests who have specially allotted places (immediate family and visitors from abroad) find them. If the bride's mother is unaccompanied when she arrives at the church an usher sees her to her seat.

Three ushers is the practical minimum. The general rule is at least one usher for each fifty guests, but as guests tend to arrive at church in a rush in the quarter of an hour before the service, it might be as well to have more. There is no point in not having plenty of ushers – some people would say you can't have too many. Usually they are friends and relations of the groom, mostly male but female too, and should include at least one connection of the bride who will be able to recognise her relations and, most importantly, her mother. In theory it is the best man's duty to give the ushers their instructions and make sure they have service sheets and seating plans, but in practice it is often the groom or even the bride who does this.

STAGE 3 CHECKLIST

Starting 3 or 4 weeks before wedding

◇ Go over Stage 2 Checklist and do anything you have forgotten

◇ Check groom has Certificate of Banns, tickets for honeymoon, etc.

◇ Telephone florist, caterer, car company, photographer, musicians, etc. and confirm details

◇ Have cars serviced

◇ Check groom has chosen ushers

◇ Draw up timetable for the day

◇ Prepare speech if making one

◇ Have hair cut

◇ Telephone guests who haven't replied

◇ Confirm numbers with caterer

◇ Decorate cake

◇ Draw up seating plan for church and table plan for reception

◇ Order flowers from you to your mother and mother-in-law

◇ Practise journey to church

◇ Pack honeymoon suitcase

◇ Check progress of reception decorations, food, etc.

◇ Attend wedding rehearsal

◇ Make sure you get plenty of rest

THE BEST MAN

The best man is usually the groom's brother (or sister) or best friend and the choice is really your fiancé's. But if he isn't sure whom to ask he might consult you, in which case it would be as well to have thought about it. The ideal best man is someone who is tactful, responsible, resourceful, has imagination and a sense of humour. He is also a superb public speaker. Not many best men fit the bill exactly – far from it. Even a very imperfect best man can make all the difference to the smoothness of the day's events, however. He has to be the groom's eyes and ears, acting on his behalf in all practical matters, because the groom himself will be too distracted and busy to deal with issues like getting Great-Aunt Mabel to the reception after the service.

One other qualification which the best man should have is that he should generally be of the same religion as that in which the marriage is being celebrated. If your fiancé is Christian and his best friend is Jewish, for example, it might be tactless to ask him to be best man. Instead, your fiancé could tell him how sorry he is that it isn't appropriate to ask him, but invite him to be an usher instead (if the friend is able to attend the wedding). In a close family, two brothers could share the job of best man, being 'supporters' or 'groomsmen'. Both stand at the chancel steps, one taking charge of the ring, and the other or both making a speech at the reception.

HELPING THE BEST MAN

So that he knows exactly what is going on during your wedding day, your fiancé's best man should be kept in touch with arrangements before the day. During the last month, you could telephone him once a week with a progress report. It will help him if you supply him with the following at least a week before the wedding:

► List of all important people such as your parents, the minister (so he can call him to arrange payments), the chief bridesmaid, etc., with their addresses and telephone numbers
► Names of the ushers
► Copies of the seating plan for your side of the church
► List of formal photographs you want taken
► Copy of the family tree you have drawn up for the photographer
► Detailed maps (if he has not already received these with his invitation)

If your fiancé and his best man are travelling some distance and need to spend the night before the wedding nearby, you could arrange for them to stay with friends of yours or your parents where they will be in a friendlier environment than a hotel, however pleasant, could offer. If they arrive in your area in good time the previous day, it will help the best man if you can take him on a short tour of all important locations – your parents' home, the church or place of worship, the reception – before the rehearsal. At the church, show him where to find the service sheets the next day.

RESPONSIBILITIES

The best man plays an important role on the day of the wedding, but he also has responsibilities in advance of the wedding day which fall into four categories: the 'stag' night or weekend, his speech, the ring and the groom.

It is usual for the groom to have a party, either one evening or over a weekend, a few weeks before the wedding, for a select few male friends. The best man usually organises this in consultation with the groom. The received image of a stag night is of gluttony, drunkenness and boisterous behaviour, but not all grooms-to-be are inclined towards this type of over-indulgence. A civilised dinner with some witty speeches held at a club, someone's home or at a restaurant suits some men better. Others prefer a weekend in the country, staying at a rented cottage, going for invigorating walks, spending the evenings in pubs and generally getting away from the pressures of everyday life. The best man should discuss various alternatives with the groom, and find out who he wants to invite, before organising the event.

The best man has to decide whether his speech is going to be off the cuff or thoroughly researched and well rehearsed. Off-the-cuff speeches should only be made by proficient and experienced speakers with plenty of self-confidence, and they should be kept very short. In general it is safer for the best man to research and practise his speech. Let him know how big the reception room or marquee will be and whether there will be a microphone so that he can practise his speech at a suitable volume. If you know any comic stories about your fiancé which you think would be suitable in the best man's speech, suggest them to him, but not in such a way that he feels obliged to incorporate them. You should also discuss with him who will deliver the telemessages to him and when, for him to read out at the reception. If you have any particular requests about the telemessages – that you would like him to read the place or country each one has been sent from and the name of the sender rather than reading out the entire messages, for example – explain this to him.

Traditionally the best man has nightmares about the ring. Will he be able to keep it safe until the wedding? Will he remember to take it to church? Will he drop it down a grating at the vital moment? In fact, he invariably manages to look after it until handing it over safely at the right point in the service, but the worries are almost obligatory. Fortunately for you, they are *his* worries. Once the ring has been bought and handed over to him you can forget about it. If the worst did happen, a married woman in the congregation – your mother perhaps – could always lend you her ring during the ceremony pending retrieval or replacement of your own wedding ring. Make sure you have your ring insured when you buy it.

Together with the ring, the most important of the best man's responsibilities is the groom himself, who should be at church (or the place of worship) about half an hour before the service, well groomed and correctly dressed. A great deal of preparatory work goes into this apparently simple event. The groom needs the right type of clothes (taking his lead from the bride's father) and they need to fit and be spotlessly clean. The same goes for the appearance of the best man. The checklist below applies equally to the best man as it does to the groom (except for honeymoon requirements). Every detail needs to be checked, down to the soles of the groom's shoes. When he kneels in church, these will be visible to the congregation. The buttonholes for groom and best man will probably be delivered to the bride's parents' home with the other flowers and need to be retrieved at a prearranged time or delivery organised.

GROOMING

The best man should make himself responsible for details of his and the groom's personal appearance such as hair cut, short clean nails, clean hands and a smooth shave. Some department stores and barber shops offer male grooming consultations, and his forthcoming wedding might give your fiancé and his best man the courage to have a go at something they have never considered before.

BEST MAN'S GROOM CHECKLIST

Since it is the custom for marriages to take place from the bride's home rather than her fiancé's, the groom is likely to be travelling and staying away for the night before his wedding and will need the best man's help in remembering all the necessary items of clothing and documentation.

- Wedding ring or rings (if best man hasn't already got it/them safely)
- Morning coat and trousers
- Waistcoat
- Shirt and tie
- Dark socks
- Clean handkerchiefs and underwear
- Cufflinks, tie pin
- Watch that works and is accurate
- Clean black shoes with clean soles
- Clothes brush
- Umbrella
- Mackintosh or coat
- Shaving and washing things including nailbrush, deodorant and shampoo
- Hairbrush or comb
- Nail scissors or clippers
- Spare spectacles
- Suit for going away
- Black-tie clothes for evening party
- Shirt and tie for going away/evening
- Socks and shoes for going away/evening
- Certificate of Banns (if not already delivered to the minister)
- Copies of the seating plan for his side of the church
- Notes for speech
- Small notebook and pencil for last-minute additions to speech, etc.
- Tickets, passport, maps, etc., for honeymoon
- Honeymoon clothes and equipment, e.g., swimming things or walking boots, camera and film, packed except for washing things in current use
- Suitcase for morning clothes, etc., to be left with the best man when bride and groom have gone on their honeymoon

LEGAL PREPARATIONS

Marriages in the United Kingdom fall into two categories for the purposes of legal preliminaries: those celebrated according to the rites of the Church of England, and all others which means *all* Roman Catholic, Nonconformist, non-Christian and register-office weddings. In these cases civil preliminaries must be fulfilled at your local register office before the marriage can take place. In the Church of England, these preliminaries have been absorbed into the church's own procedures, since it is the established church of the land. If you are getting married in a Church of England church but one of you is a member of another Church, you do not have to complete the civil preliminaries at a register office.

The legal preliminaries are very straightforward for most people and involve little more than filling out a few forms with such detail as your names, date of birth, and some information about your father. There are certain blood relatives and relations by marriage whom you may not legally marry, but problems arising from these laws are rare. Ideally, you should produce your birth certificate for the registrar, but your passport or other proof of identity may be satisfactory. If you have been married previously, you will have to show a death or divorce certificate to the minister to prove that you are free to marry again. If you are under 18, your parents or guardians will have to give their permission in writing, unless you are a widow or widower or marrying in Scotland, which has its own rules governing register office and all other weddings. (The best advice is to always contact your local registrar or minister who will be able to give you the correct details for your particular circumstances.)

To be legally binding, a marriage must include a declaration by both people being married, in front of each other and two other adult witnesses, that they are free to marry. This is followed by a spoken contract between them that they will become husband and wife. The declaration and contract must be included in the wording of every religious marriage service. Immediately after this the marriage is registered – in the Church of England by the person who has just conducted the marriage and in other places of worship by a person licensed to register marriages. The name of the denomination by whose rites you were married is included on the registration form for all religious marriages.

There are two forms of civil marriage authorisation: the Superintendent Registrar's Certificate Without Licence, and the same but With Licence. The former requires 21 days between the date of notice being given by you at the register office and the certificate being issued, and you both have to give notice at your local offices; the latter requires only one clear day other than a Sunday, Christmas Day or Good Friday, and only one of you has to give notice. Once you have a certificate you can make an appointment to be married in your local register office on any day except Sundays, Christmas Day or Good Friday.

One area of confusion which sometimes arises in Church of England weddings concerns the question of who can be married in which church. The rules are that you can, almost without exception, be married in the church of the parish in which you live, by your parish priest, after the calling of banns. Banns are a public announcement of your intention to marry. The minister includes them amongst his other weekly notices and says, 'I publish the banns of marriage between Catherine Jennifer Smith, of this parish, and Angus George Carey, of the parish of St Mary, Little Salton. If any of you know cause, or just impediment, why these two persons should not be joined together in Holy Matrimony, ye are to declare it.' Banns are called on three Sundays, not necessarily successive, within the three-month period before the wedding.

If your parish church is not your local church or the church where you regularly worship, or if you wish to be married in your parents' parish church you can, after consultation with the clergyman and with his consent, either join the electoral roll and be married by banns, or apply for a licence to be married there. The electoral roll gives parishioners' rights (including that of being married) to people who aren't parishioners, and you have to have worshipped regularly in a church for six months to be eligible to join its electoral roll.

There are two types of licence: Common and Special. Both forms free you from the necessity of calling banns. A Common Licence is generally granted by the diocesan office to people who need to avoid publicity or where there is insufficient time to call banns before the wedding, but it is valid only for marriage in your parish church. If you want to be married elsewhere, you will need a Special Licence granted at the discretion of the Archbishop of Canterbury. Most applications for these come from people who want to be married from their parents' home in the local church, and many of the rest enable people to be married in places of worship which are not registered for marriage, such as university, school and hospital chapels.

There is one other, exceptional, way of being married in the Church of England, and that is following civil rather than ecclesiastical preliminaries, by way of a Certificate of the Superintendent Registrar of Marriages. Such certificates are rarely granted or used, and only in very unusual circumstances such as in the case of the marriage of a divorced person.

Weddings abroad are increasingly popular, and there are several travel companies which organise these. The embassy or consulate for the country concerned, and the travel company, should help you ensure that you fulfil all necessary legal requirements for marriage in your destination country. So long as the form of your marriage ceremony complies with the law of the country where you are married, the marriage will generally be recognised in this country.

One of the ways in which marriage affects a woman but not a man is in the still-current expectation that she will abandon her surname and adopt her husband's. There is no legal requirement for her to do so and women increasingly prefer not to. Some women add their husband's name to their own, as in Mary Parker Jones, or their husband may take their name, or they may combine both into a double-barrelled name. More frequently, however, a

woman with professional or business interests chooses to continue with the name that has become her 'trademark', for work and financial matters, even if she adopts her husband's surname for family matters. If you intend to continue to use your own name, the only person you need to tell is your tax collector, at the same time informing him of your tax arrangements with your husband (do this anyway). Consult your accountant about the alternative tax arrangements for married couples.

If you do choose to adopt your husband's name, you become the equivalent of Mrs Henry Fairfax (Mrs Anne Fairfax indicates a divorcee). You should inform anyone with whom you have legal, financial or professional arrangements of your change of name. These might include: your employer, your accountant, solicitor, banks, building societies, credit card companies, store accounts, insurance companies, pension schemes, clubs, doctors and dentists. Prepare a standard letter and send it out at the same time to them all, keeping a record of whom you have written to. You should also change your driving licence, vehicle documents and your passport (this can be done in advance and postdated: see page 205). If you keep your own name, you could forestall complications in the future by keeping a certified copy (a photocopy won't do) of your marriage certificate with your passport.

Before you get married, you might like to consider making a will. If you already have one, it becomes invalid when you marry. A will made before marriage is valid after marriage if it incorporates the words 'made in contemplation of my

forthcoming marriage to. . .' (and the name of your fiancé). If you don't make a will and you die intestate, what happens to your estate follows complicated rules which depend on how much you leave and who you leave behind in terms of relatives. If you and your husband die together, the younger is deemed to have survived the older, so your combined estates pass to the relatives of whichever of you is younger. It all sounds chilling – perhaps the best thing is to make a new will 'in contemplation of marriage' and then forget about the whole business.

FINAL CHECKLIST

On the day

◇ Sleep in

◇ Have a relaxing bath

◇ Check flowers for you and your attendants have arrived or are on their way

◇ Eat a good breakfast

◇ Give attendants their presents

◇ Don't drink too much fluid

◇ Transfer engagement ring to your right hand

◇ Get dressed

◇ Relax and enjoy yourself

INVITATIONS

A wedding invitation is like any other in that it should carry clear information about the event to which the guest is being invited and by whom. The information comes in two forms. More obviously, it tells you certain facts such as who is marrying whom, where, on what day and at what time, followed by what sort of celebration and where, where to reply to and, usually, who your hosts are. More subtly, its appearance and the 'tone of voice' in which the factual information is expressed tell you something about the style of the wedding.

WHAT THE INVITATION SAYS

If the invitation is a severely elegant stiff plain upright white card doubled back, with clear black 'curly' script print raised slightly from the page, you know it is a traditional formal wedding to which you should wear morning dress (gentlemen) or a smart dress or suit and a hat (ladies). If a brightly coloured hand-printed request that you should 'come to our wedding' lands on your doormat, you can tell that the event is going to be a jazzier affair.

Don't dismiss the elegant black and white invitation, however. Since the invitations are sent, in normal circumstances, by the bride's parents they may have insisted on a conventional form of invitation while all other aspects of the wedding have been arranged by their daughter, an artistic girl with colourful ideas which are far from conventional. On the other hand, many people opt for the classic invitation because it is simple and handsome to look at, its

dignity is in keeping with the importance of the event, and it is the conventional form for what is, after all, a very conventional occasion.

A traditional style of invitation to a wedding followed by a reception is shown on the opposite page. This tells you everything you need to know, down to the fact that the reception is not being held at the bride's parents' home but at the college or school in their local town. What it does not tell you is exactly who is paying for what. Even if the groom's parents are paying half the cost, the invitation still comes from the bride's parents. The groom's parents' contribution is acknowledged in the speeches not the invitation.

RSVP

Literally this means 'répondez s'il vous plaît', French for 'please reply'. This is printed in the bottom left-hand corner of the invitation, with the address to reply to underneath. No name is necessary, unless the person to whom you should reply is different to the person whose name appears at the top of the invitation (replies are sent to the wife only). If the invitation is impersonal and is worded 'The pleasure of your company is requested . . .', a name should be given under RSVP. It is courteous to reply as soon as you receive the invitation and certainly no later than a fortnight before the wedding. If you receive a telephone call from the hosts in the final week you should apologise for not replying and, ideally, have a good reason such as your absence abroad until the day before the call. If the uncertainty of events such as an ill-

ness in the family prevent your knowing if you can accept until very near the date, telephone or write to your hosts as soon as you receive your invitation, explaining this and asking if you could delay a definite reply until then. Specify a date by which you will let them know one way or the other. They have seating and catering arrangements to make. If the invitation is to a couple or family it is quite in order for one or more persons to accept and the others to refuse.

Alternative wordings

There are frequently family complications which mean that the hosts are not the bride's married parents. They may be divorced but hosting the wedding together, or one parent may be dead, or a natural parent and their second spouse may be hosts. If the situation is exceptionally complicated it may be best for the invitation to be worded impersonally:

The pleasure of your company
is requested at
the marriage of
Mary Catherine Scott
to
Mr Gareth Alwyn Jones

etc.

This form of invitation is also a possibility if you and your fiancé are yourselves acting as hosts at your own wedding. However there is almost certainly a form of words which states who the hosts are and probably also defines their relationship to the bride (see page 53).

Rank, qualifications and titles

If the groom is an army officer his rank appears instead of 'Mr' and the name of his regiment is included below and in slightly smaller type than his name, to the right of centre. In the case of the other armed forces, the letters 'RN' or 'RAF' are included after the groom's name. If the groom is a doctor, or has a title, this is included on the invitation but no letters appear after his name. No other qualifications appear on the invitation. Only the bride's Christian name or names appear, not her rank, title or qualifications. If the bride is a widow, the words 'widow of . . .' and the name of her first husband can be included below her name.

Dress

It is often asked whether it is correct for the type of dress to be printed in the bottom right-hand corner of the invitation. The answer is that it is not – information about what the men in particular should wear is passed by word of mouth. The groom's best man and father dress in the same manner as the bride's father and the groom, with other men either following suit or choosing between their usual attire for weddings and smart lounge suits.

WORDING FOR ALTERNATIVE OCCASIONS

The format of a formal invitation can be adapted to any variation of wedding celebrations (see adjacent examples).

Mr and Mrs Adrian Peck
request the pleasure of
your company at the marriage
of their daughter
Anna
to
Mr Gregory Hamilton
at St Mary's Church
Green Pond, Staveley,
on Saturday, 3rd April, 1992
at 3 o'clock and afterwards at
The White Swan Staveley

R.S.V.P
138 Rosebery Road
Staveley, Yorks

TRADITIONAL

Mr and Mrs Richard Lewis
request the pleasure of your company
at a Service of Blessing
following the marriage
of their daughter
Jane
to
Mr Simon Starr
at All Saints' Church, Norwich,
on Saturday, 9th September, 1992
at 3 o'clock and afterwards at
The White House, Norwich

R.S.V.P
19 York Way
Norwich

SERVICE OF BLESSING

Mr and Mrs George Bellamy
request the pleasure of
your company at a reception
following the marriage
of their daughter
Julie
to
Mr Michael Horner
at The White House, Hindhead
on Saturday, 24th March, 1992
at 12 o'clock

R.S.V.P
23 Acacia Avenue
Hindhead

RECEPTION

Mr and Mrs Peter Collins
at Home
to celebrate the marriage
of their daughter
Sarah
to
Mr John Smith
on Saturday, 17th July, 1992
at 8 o'clock

R.S.V.P
17 Ruskin Avenue
Leyton
Dorset

EVENING DANCE
(in lieu of reception)

Evening dance

If an evening dance is the main celebration following a wedding, in lieu of a reception or other party, the invitation can be printed on folded card, in the same format as a wedding invitation.

At home

An invitation to a dance in the evening following a day-time wedding is issued on a separate card by the host or hosts for the party, in the usual format for a formal invitation. The host may be different from the hosts for the wedding. If your parents are hosts, the invitation generally comes from your mother only.

The term 'at Home' is used on formal invitations even if the party is not taking place in the person's home but in reception rooms at another location such as a club or hotel. The alternative to a formal invitation is an informal party invitation of any design that you like.

If the dance follows on directly from a late afternoon reception it would be inappropriate to issue a separate invitation, but you will want your guests to understand what is involved and that the party will go on later than it would if it were simply a reception or meal. In this case you should add the words

supper

dancing

in the bottom right-hand corner of the wedding invitation.

A bride hosting a reception following her own second wedding might feel it more appropriate to issue 'at Home' cards rather than full-blown wedding invitations. The wording would be: 'Mrs Philippa Douglas at Home following her marriage to Mr Crispin Chambers on . . .'

HOW MANY?

When ordering invitations remember that you only need one per couple and family with young children, but order a few extra in case of accident.

DESIGN OF THE INVITATIONS

The plain white upright card folded double is an echo of an earlier era. Until the Second World War, all fine writing paper was folded in this way for ordinary letters. But shortages during the war years led the government of the day to ban such folded paper by statute. However short the letter, the paper was always folded double, even if the second page was not written on, and this was considered a waste. The traditional wedding invitation's formal wording and script, in black on white, provides a wonderfully economical method of communicating a large amount of information in a small space. Unfortunately, high-street newsagents and stationery shops do not in general offer this classic invitation format amongst the standard stock that they will print for you at very reasonable cost. It is usually necessary to go to an old-fashioned printer or a city-centre stationer to find the right quality of traditional materials, design and printing. Not too old-fashioned though, since new and cheaper methods of producing raised print have superceded the engraving process.

The strictly traditional form of invitation can successfully be varied by choosing a tinted card – cream, palest blue or green, for example – and lettering which is clear and classic but different to the usual italic upper- and lower-case script. A good printer will be able to show you a selection of lettering styles. Alternatively, the formal wording of the traditional wedding invitation could be used but arranged in a different format, perhaps in a neat column below a printed classical swag. Or the usual white folded card could be fixed on the left or in the top corner with a coloured ribbon. Whatever your invitation looks like, make sure you get an estimate of the cost and give the printer accurate information about what wording is to appear, in what format. It is vital to see a proof before giving him the go-ahead. Check the proof carefully, taking your time and looking at every single word, date, number and punctuation mark. Show it to a friend, as a fresh pair of eyes may spot a mistake you missed through familiarity.

You could abandon the traditional form altogether, in favour of a simple mass-produced invitation card or, preferably, something which reflects your personal style and individual wedding. If money is a problem, handmade invitations are sometimes preferable to most readily available manufactured invitations, which tend to be sentimental and sometimes overstate the obvious by having the words 'Wedding Invitation' printed ostentatiously on the front. Perhaps the most unusual and original wedding invitation is a limited edition print created by a local artist or artist friend, which your guests will want to keep and frame as a memento of your wedding. Make sure that the artist has exact details of the information to appear (including date and spellings), that you like the preliminary designs he prepares for you, and that he gives you (in writing) an accurate estimate of what everything will cost, including envelopes. Alternatively, you could commission a calligrapher to write out the wording of the invitation and have this reproduced on card. In the end this is a matter of personal taste which will reflect your wedding style.

DRAWING UP THE LIST

The guest list is usually the bride's mother's responsibility and is a special area of potential contention and embarrassment. The groom's parents need to be informed at an early stage how many guests they may invite (half the total, unless one or other family or circle of close friends is extraordinarily large in which case some diplomacy and negotiation will be necessary). You and your mother, meanwhile, have the unfortunate task of reducing your combined guest list to the right num-

ber. It is not unusual for the initial list to be two or three times the required length. Invite a few more people than you have room for – some will refuse. The usual estimated refusal rate is a quarter.

Decide amicably whether the emphasis is going to be on family and parents' friends or on your contemporaries, or, as is usually the case, a balance between the two. If it's to be a 'young' wedding, or if your parents have a wide circle of friends, they could give a party for their contemporaries soon after the wedding, at which you and your new husband would appear in your going-away outfits. Your parents could serve champagne and show the video (if you have one). If parents' friends take precedence, don't be embarrassed quietly to warn anyone you won't be asking that you are very sorry you can't invite them because of limited numbers. They should appreciate your frankness and expression of regret. If you don't mention it you may find you feel guilty about it every time you see them, before and after the wedding.

Choosing who to ask and who not to ask can be a painful business if you have many close friends. The fact that a friend invited you to her wedding is not a good enough reason in itself for you to feel you should ask her (and her husband) to yours. She may have had a larger wedding than you, or not have so many close friends. Think of a wedding invitation as a bond for the future. You found it a moving experience and an honour to be at a friend's wedding, and you want the people who share your wedding with you to have the same attitude. If there are people on your first draft guest list who you feel expect to be asked

for purely social reasons or whose attitude to your marriage service will be one of superior cynicism, consider crossing them off first. Otherwise, the simplest criterion for drawing the line is gut feeling. Who would you really mind *not* being there?

If your guest list has to be cut radically (not unusual) another method is to invite one member of a family to represent the whole family, and explain what you've done and why. Everyone who has been through it understands the difficulty of pruning the guest list. You could lend the other members of the family a copy of the video afterwards or go round some time afterwards with the photographs or both.

The guest list includes your and your fiancé's attendants, including best man and ushers, your fiancé's parents, the person officiating at the wedding if it is a religious service and their spouse. People whom you know are unable to come but who are close friends or relatives are also sent invitations. The guest list does not, traditionally, include the groom himself, who is presumed to know about his own wedding. But if he would like an invitation for the fun of it, there's no reason why he can't have one.

Your guest list need not include your friends' current boy- or girl-friends, especially if you have not met them. Don't allow your friends to pressurise you on this point. A guest list is usually a finite number, not endlessly elastic. If you invite their friend, however special he or she is, it means you can invite one less of your own friends. Likewise, don't let your parents and their friends take over completely – it is your wedding not theirs.

If a couple is living together or is of very

long standing, and you know them both well, you will probably want to invite them both anyway. Engaged couples should be treated exactly as married couples, and if a guest becomes engaged after the invitations have been sent you can write or telephone and suggest they bring their fiancé. If you don't, they may telephone you and it is courteous to agree, unless there is a specific reason why you cannot.

ADDRESSING YOUR GUESTS

The name of the person invited is handwritten in the top left-hand corner of the printed invitation: *'Mr George Saunders'*. If a couple, their names are written 'Mr and Mrs George Saunders', but the envelope is addressed only to Mrs George Saunders. Young children's Christian names only are added: 'Mr and Mrs George Saunders, Emily and Kate'. If their names are not added this indicates that they are not expected. Older children's names appear in full: 'Mr James Saunders, Miss Catherine Saunders'. Offspring over the age of 18 or 21 (a matter of taste) are often sent their own invitations, certainly if they have moved away from home to work or study. It is irritating never to see your invitation because your name has been added to your parents', even though you live for most of the year at the other end of the country. Apart from anything else, if you have not been sent your invitation you cannot check the details of times and places.

A divorced woman, currently single, is addressed as 'Mrs Sarah Bolton', but a widow carries her husband's name: 'Mrs

Mark Jenkins'. Both names of an engaged couple or an established couple who are not married but live together appear on the invitation; the envelope is addressed in the former case to your friend, whether the man or the woman (both if you know them both), and in the latter case to the woman, as if they were married.

The envelope is addressed to the wife if the guests are married. In all other cases, for example, brothers and sisters, it is addressed to the people whose names appear on the invitation, but excludes the names of small children. If the guest is titled, is a Member of Parliament or has some other handle to his or her name, the full designation appears on the envelope, but the invitation has the shortened version of their name. In the case of almost all titles, the wife's name adopts the rank of her husband, and the envelope is addressed to her

alone: 'Lady George Meredith', 'The Hon. Mrs James Lucas'. The exception is bishops, who sit in the House of Lords while their wives remain commoners. If the wife has a title in her own right, she retains it and her husband remains as he was before marriage: 'Mr Philip and Lady Lilias Denby'.

SENDING INVITATIONS

Your parents are responsible for this, and invitations should all be sent at the same time, between a month and two months before the wedding. Six weeks is a fair time before the event – if you leave it too late your guests may have prior engagements. With so many envelopes to address, you or your parents should start writing them well in advance of the date upon which they are to be sent.

REPLIES

Sometimes a printed reply card is enclosed with the invitation, but many people who receive these consider them a cold and unfriendly way of responding to a wedding invitation and will handwrite a reply. This is especially likely if the invitee has to refuse and wishes to do so graciously, stating a reason, rather than merely deleting, 'as applicable', sections of a postcard. An acceptance or refusal of a formal wedding invitation is written in the third person:

12 View Rise
Great Plimpton
Gloucestershire

Mr and Mrs George Smith thank Mr and Mrs Alexander Marshall for their kind invitation to the marriage of their daughter Katriona at St Cecilia's, Plumhampton, on Saturday 26th August and afterwards at Calsham Court and have great pleasure in accepting.

If you have to refuse it is courteous to give a reason:

Miss Joanna Cavendish thanks Mr and Mrs Leigh Verran for their kind invitation to the marriage of their daughter Fiona on Saturday, 24th April and much regrets that she is unable to accept because she has a long-standing business engagement abroad on the Friday evening and cannot return in time to attend the wedding.

ALTERNATIVE WORDING

BRIDE'S DIVORCED PARENTS, FATHER POSSIBLY REMARRIED:
Mr Brian Acton and Mrs Joan Acton . . . at the marriage of their daughter Anne . . .

BRIDE'S DIVORCED PARENTS, MOTHER REMARRIED AND FATHER POSSIBLY REMARRIED:
Mr James Packland and Mrs Michael Finn . . . at the marriage of their daughter Caroline . . .

BRIDE'S FATHER AND STEPMOTHER
Mr and Mrs Edward Stewart . . . at the marriage of his daughter Serena . . .

BRIDE'S MOTHER AND STEPFATHER
Mr and Mrs Charles Anderson . . . at the marriage of her daughter Felicity . . .
It is acceptable for Felicity's own surname to appear if she would like it to. This is not 'traditional' but neither is the divorce rate

BRIDE'S WIDOWED AND REMARRIED MOTHER
Mr and Mrs Alfred Morris . . . at the marriage of her daughter Georgina
Georgina's surname can appear, or the words 'daughter of the late Mr Philip Gough' could be included in the line below her name, if it is important to her that her father's name appears on the invitation

ONE PARENT OF THE BRIDE
Mrs John Acres . . . at the marriage of her daughter Jane . . .

OTHER RELATIVES OF THE BRIDE
Mr and Mrs Nicholas Baker . . . at the marriage of his niece Miranda . . .
Replace 'his' with 'her' and 'niece' with any other relationship as appropriate. Miranda's surname may be included

PROXY PARENTS OF THE BRIDE, DISTANT RELATIONS OR NO BLOOD RELATION
Mr and Mrs Laurence Maitland . . . at the marriage of Kate, daughter of the late Mr and Mrs Andrew Hodge . . .

GROOM'S PARENTS
Mr and Mrs Angus Hartley . . . at the marriage of Miss Philippa Cathcart to their son Mr William Hartley . . .
Or Philippa, daughter of the late Mr and Mrs Donald Cathcart

BRIDE AND GROOM
Miss Helen Milne and Mr Piers Allison . . . at their marriage . . .

PARENTS HOSTS AT A DOUBLE WEDDING
Mr and Mrs Patrick Brown . . . at the marriage of their daughters Claire to Mr Simon Wilding and Lucy to Mr Jonathan Lundy . . .

On the continent and for Jewish weddings the invitation is usually issued by both sets of parents. For a register-office wedding or a very small wedding with, say, twenty guests, it is usual to handwrite the invitation.

SERVICE SHEETS

Service sheets are a guide to the order of service for everyone present at your marriage in church. They save time and trouble in church and allow those present to concentrate on the service itself. Many of your guests will keep their service sheet as a memento of your wedding, and the sheets from friends' weddings will be a useful source of possible music, hymns and lessons for your own service.

The service sheet is traditionally an upright white folded card, similar to the wedding invitation but possibly of lighter weight. The name of the church and the town, the date and time, and your and your fiancé's initials or names are printed on the front (yours at bottom left, his at bottom right). Inside, the music, hymns, lessons, prayers, address and the marriage itself are listed in the order in which they will happen, with some indication of what they are, composed or written by whom, given or sung by whom and a few helpful indicators like 'All shall kneel'. In order for this information to fit on the three remaining pages of a single folded card it is usually not much more than a list, with the exception of the hymns and responses which appear in full so that everyone can join in.

Service sheets are generally printed in black on white, with a clear classic typeface that is easily legible. Your service sheet need not be totally plain, although the contents should always be clear and easy to read. It need not be so short: you might like to include the words of songs sung during the signing of the register, prayers, and even the Lord's Prayer. You may have known it by heart since you were six but it might not be familiar to friends of another

faith and visitors from abroad. It will draw everyone who is present together, if they can all join in speaking this beautiful prayer. A service sheet can run to as many pages as you wish, and have a coloured decorated cover, all attached by staple or coloured ribbon. You could have inside pages handwritten and photocopied, and assemble them yourself inside a printed cover, secured with ribbon.

The cover could be coloured card, or show the church where the service is held, another building or place of significance to you and your fiancé, or your initials could be wreathed in flowers like a page from a Victorian poetry book. The cover could be framed with sprigs of plants with relevant meanings: myrtle for love, for example, ivy for friendship, fidelity and marriage, and rosemary for remembrance. Why not use your imagination and have an image or

create a symbolism relevant to you, rather than succumb to the popularised sentimentality of silver horse shoes and wedding bells.

Draw or design the cover yourself if you can, or get a friend or relative to do it. Or you could commission a local artist or illustrator. Check first with the printer about the form and size in which he will want the artwork. Before undertaking any of this, you should follow the usual rule of researching costs and satisfying yourself (or the person in charge of the budget) that you can afford what you want. Some people might consider money spent in this way to be an extravagance, but a beautifully designed and printed service sheet will always be a potent reminder and record of your wedding. Whether or not it is worth it probably depends upon your own feelings about the importance of the service itself.

When calculating how many to have printed, allow one service sheet for each guest, one for each attendant and officiant, one for each member of the choir, one for the organist, and one each for you and your fiancé. You may like to have some extra to send to people who cannot come, including relations abroad, and you should order an extra dozen or two to be on the safe side. Before ordering check that the information you give the printer is correct in every detail of spelling, dates and punctuation, and show it to your minister. His help is invaluable in that he will be able to see at a glance if something is out of place or events are in the wrong order. There is nothing more confusing than having to announce a change in the order of service once the service has begun.

PHOTOGRAPHS AND VIDEO

The ideal coverage of a wedding combines a record of who was there and what happened with an impression of the mood of the occasion. Photographs and video can each play a part, and these days it is quite usual to have both. Together they are an expensive and risky element of your wedding. So much seems to depend upon what happens on the day. In fact, as much depends upon the quality of raw material such as the video company's equipment, efficiency and, most important of all, the quality of the cameraman's photography. This an area where it can be dangerous to economise. You should buy the best you can afford.

Ways of finding photographers and video companies to research include word of mouth, classified advertisements in wedding magazines and local papers, and the British Institute of Professional Photography (Tel: 0920 464011), the Society of Wedding Photographers (Tel: 0372 726122) and the Guild of Wedding Photographers (Tel: 061 926 9367) which issue a list of their members. Whoever you choose, put all your instructions in writing, adding politely that your purchase of the pictures or video is subject to their being of an acceptable standard.

PHOTOGRAPHS

Photographers use various terms which you may be unfamiliar with, and they generally offer various packages at different prices. Some will attend your wedding without charge and with no guarantee from you of how many prints you will buy. Others want an attendance fee and deposit on prints. A print is a copy of a photograph. A proof is a numbered print, circulated to you, your parents and your fiancé's parents for them to see before deciding if they want to buy a copy. A contact sheet is a page of small prints from which you choose the ones you want blown up. 'Square', 'portrait' and 'landscape' are terms referring to the shape of the print.

Packages vary hugely. Some include attendance and a set number of prints chosen by the photographer, perhaps mounted in an album. Others give you a certain number of prints chosen by you from proofs or contact sheets. Some include photographs at your home before the wedding and some don't. Some include the services of an assistant who will take informal shots of the guests at the reception. Many people find the albums offered by photographers are not to their taste. Have a good look at what is available in the shops before you agree to a photographer's package including album, and be sure you wouldn't rather have more prints for the money and save up for a really beautiful album later.

VIDEO

There are two excellent reasons for having a video. The first is that your wedding day will pass by in a flash of happiness and a blur of faces. This is especially true of the marriage service itself. The video will give you the chance to relive it, moment by moment, savouring it all in your own time. Your relatives abroad who can't come, not to mention your children and grandchildren, will bless you for having the video so that they too can enjoy it in retro-spect. The other reason is that while you are signing the register you are missing the music being performed for your congregation, if the vestry is cut off from the church. This is especially sad if a friend or relation is performing, perhaps as their wedding present to you. The video, even more than a sound recording, will bring this to life again for you.

The only question remaining concerns the propriety of filming a religious service, and this is largely a matter of taste, depending on your own feelings and the attitude of the person conducting the service. Ask the minister for his views, and try to persuade him if he is doubtful but doesn't actually refuse. Your enthusiasm may carry the day. The attitude of the cameraman is also important – he must want to be discreet and create no distraction from the day's important events.

When you research video companies, you need to be sure they are what they seem. It is not unknown for amateurs to pass off professionals' work as their own when touting for business. As with still photographs, ask to see work by the actual cameraman who will cover your wedding. Check that the company can secure copyright permissions and ask what happens to the master tape after the copies have been made. It may be possible to buy that too, if you want to secure it for the future.

One possible way of economising is to book the best stills photographer you can afford, and hire a video camera for a friend or relation to operate. Only do this, however, if you are happy for the result to be spontaneous to the point of being haphazard, and of ordinary technical quality.

Do's and Don'ts

DO

▶ Look at the work of several photographers and video companies before you decide, and feel free to ask questions about the techniques they use and check if they are a member of BIPP, SWP and GWP (see page 56)

▶ Book your photographer and video company as soon as possible – delay could mean disappointment as good wedding photographers and video companies and cameramen are quickly booked up for busy summer Saturdays

▶ Be sure you see examples of work by the actual photographer and cameraman who will be at your wedding, not just general studio work

▶ Ask about the various packages a photographer or video company offers, and the cost of extra prints/ tapes

▶ Ask about the cost and availability of the snapshot-size prints that are useful for sending to friends and relations around the world

▶ Remember that good photography cannot be produced cheaply – you get what you pay for and economising on photographs and video carries risks

▶ Consider having some black-and-white photographs as well as colour ones

▶ Trust your own judgement about the style of photography you like, and tell the photographer and video people. They are working for you – don't let them intimidate you

▶ Make a written list of the group shots you would like the photographer to take. Make it clear and simple – 'Mark and Mary with his parents, brothers and sisters and their families', for example, not a long list of names with no indication of who these people are

▶ Draw up a clear family tree and list of attendants so that the photographer and person organising groups knows who everyone is and what their names are (especially useful where there are divorced parents). Send this and the above list to the photographer in advance and talk to him about it

▶ Send maps, directions, information about parking, any other instructions, to photographer and video company well in advance

▶ Ensure your photographer and video company confirm the bookings in writing, quoting the time and place of your wedding, their prices and what exactly is included

▶ Give a handful of films to a friend who is a good amateur photographer and ask them to take plenty of informal shots at the reception

▶ Make sure that only one person involved in organising your wedding liaises with the photographer and video company and decides what is to be included – one of their complaints is confusion on this point and disputes arising from it

▶ Remember you don't have to smile for every photograph – better to be serene than force a grin

▶ Consider having some photographs such as informal portraits of you and your father taken the day before the wedding

DON'T

▶ Leave the quality of the photographs to chance – do your research and then you can relax on the day

▶ Assume that because a photographer or video company did a friend's wedding well they are necessarily the best for you – compare the style and location of your friend's wedding with yours

▶ Look only at the people in the photographs that a photographer has in his portfolio or the demonstration videos a company shows you – look at the technical quality, mood, composition and use of light

▶ Forget to look at all the albums the photographer offers before deciding on one. If you don't want any of his albums, ask about print-only packages or go to another photographer

▶ Let photographer's/videomaker's 'extras' take you by surprise – ask exactly what is included in the basic price and what costs more. Confirm which extras you want, in writing

▶ Rush the photographs on the day. Discuss in advance how long the photographer needs for group pictures and at what point in the day's events

▶ Expect group pictures to happen by themselves – appoint and brief a friend or relation to help the photographer assemble the right people in the right place on the day. Choose someone who won't hesitate to be bossy if this ensures you get the pictures you want, and give him or her the list of groups you gave to the photographer

▶ Assume the photographer and videomaker won't use special effects – some will automatically do 'misties' and shots which superimpose you and your fiancé onto a champagne glass, unless you make it clear you don't want them

▶ Despair if the weather is terrible – have somewhere indoors lined up as an alternative location for group photographs in case it pours/snows/ blows a gale

▶ Screw up your eyes against the sun – ask the photographer to change position

▶ Choose a photographer and videomaker you don't feel comfortable with. It's your day and they will make an important contribution to your memories of it

TIMING AND TRANSPORT

Your method of transport to the church or register office for your wedding can be as glamorous, discreet or ordinary as you like – it really doesn't matter so long as it is reliable and clean. The classic vehicle is a chauffeur-driven black or grey Bentley, Daimler or Rolls-Royce, partly because they are so roomy, but antique cars and ponies-and-traps are popular too. A spacious family car cleaned inside and out, serviced and filled with petrol and windscreen-washing fluid, is as good as anything and saves you money which you can then spend on other things.

Timing is an important practical matter, however, and the type of vehicle you use is likely to affect the amount of time you need to allow to get yourself and your father to the service. Always allow more time than you think necessary, but not too much, as you don't want to be waiting around. If possible, do a dummy run with the actual vehicle, on the same day of the week and at the same time of day as your wedding but a week or two beforehand. If the car or carriage is hired, discuss timing with the owners, who will probably have plenty of experience and be able to give a reliable estimate.

Don't forget to check on the dates of local events like carnivals or parades when calculating journeys through towns and villages. Ask your father to check on the morning of your wedding with the AA or other traffic information service about possible hold-ups caused by road repairs or accidents. The police should be told well in advance so that they can send officers to help with traffic control if they think it necessary. Remember that once the police are alerted they will also be on the look-out for drunk drivers after your reception or party – no bad thing.

Parking is a vital consideration if the day is to go smoothly and your guests are to enjoy themselves. You don't want them to spend an irritating half an hour looking for a meter when you could have told them at the start that the multistorey car park round the corner from the hotel was the quickest place to park for the reception. Ideally you should include parking information for service and reception with the invitations. You don't want to have to send out a second batch of envelopes after the acceptances have come in.

Two vehicles are usually needed; one is for your mother and the bridesmaids, the other for you and your father to travel to the service. The first car may have to make two journeys if there are lots of attendants and you live near where the ceremony is to take place. Alternatively, your mother can be driven by a friend or relative who has previously been briefed. After the service, the first car takes you and your husband to the reception and the second takes either your parents or the bridesmaids (or both, if there is room).

An open carriage or trap is a popular choice for travelling to church. Of course you will hope for glorious sunshine, but in case you aren't lucky, check that the carriage has a hood which can be put up in case of rain.

If it takes the bridesmaids only, this leaves your parents to get to the reception somehow. Either your father can have delivered their car to the church earlier, or a friend or relation should be detailed to take them to the reception. If the reception is at a place other than their home, your parents have to get home afterwards. If the second car takes your parents only, the bridesmaids can travel to the reception with their parents or with other guests, in which case the best man should be told that they need to have lifts arranged. It is his responsibility to ensure that all guests, not only the bridesmaids, have transport or a lift to the reception.

Filling in a chart with key people's names along the top and the various journeys listed down the side will help you make decisions and simplify what seems a complicated business. Don't forget that if you use a family car someone has to drive it. This is true for all vehicles, of course, but

hired ones usually come with chauffeur (check this when getting estimates and when confirming).

Research prices and book hired vehicles well in advance, especially if you have something particularly unusual or elaborate in mind. Ask about all extras, including the sort of tip the driver or drivers will expect, and the cost of flowers inside the car and ribbons and bows on the outside. Make it quite clear if you don't want these, or only want plain white ribbon, as the car-hire firm may find it difficult to believe you really do not want their lovely fancy white frills.

Practical considerations apart, your wedding gives you the opportunity to fulfil your dreams about driving in an open-top 1920s sports car, spacious and regal black Bentley, vintage yellow Rolls-Royce, or travelling by brewer's horse and brightly painted dray. So long as it fits into the budget and your dress fits into it without

getting wet, dirty or crushed, let fantasy rule. Here is a list of some possible forms of transport for getting you to and from the service:

Black or grey Bentley, Daimler or Rolls-Royce
Black taxi
Yellow New York cab
Red London bus
Vintage car (made 1917-30)
Veteran car (made 1916 or earlier)
1920s open sports car
1950s pink Cadillac convertible
Horse-drawn carriage
Pony and open trap
Brewer's horse and dray

Going away clothes are more versatile than wedding dresses, on the whole, so the vehicle in or on which you travel for the first part of your honeymoon journey can be wilder still (see pages 198-199).

Veteran and vintage cars are fun but have antique suspension so aren't as smooth as modern ones. They also move quite slowly, so allow a few minutes extra in your time-table calculations for your wedding day.

3

THE MARRIAGE

THE GROOM, BEST MAN AND USHERS ON THE DAY

BEST MAN

The wedding day is a busy one for the best man. Here is an outline of things to do:

► Check groom is up in good time
► Check going-away car is clean
► Check the car has petrol and windscreen-washing fluid
► Take groom's going-away things and going-away car to reception location
► Collect buttonholes or check they will be at the church
► Check service sheets at church
► Meet ushers for lunch with groom (if an afternoon wedding) and brief them
► Give ushers seating plans for both sides of church and explain where service sheets are
► Get self completely ready and check wedding ring(s)
► Make sure the groom is ready and has every little thing he needs
► Get groom to church in good time
► Ensure fees are paid at church
► Look after groom's top hat if he has one
► Stand with groom on bride's right at chancel steps until the marriage part of the service is over, producing ring(s) at the right moment
► Retire to first pew
► Go to vestry for the signing
► Either remain in vestry for practical arrangements or escort chief bridesmaid down the aisle in the recession
► Ensure everyone has lifts to the reception
► Help organise people to appear in photographs
► At reception, announce the cutting of the cake if there is no Master of Ceremonies
► Introduce the speakers
► Make speech after the groom, thanking groom on behalf of the bridesmaids for his toast to them
► At all times, take the initiative (without being officious), as the bride and groom won't be in a state of mind to deal with practicalities

GROOM

Much the same guidelines apply to the groom as to the bride on the wedding day: get a good night's sleep, have a luxurious soak in the bath, eat a hearty breakfast, don't drink much (ideally, no alcohol) in the hours before the wedding, get dressed carefully and, most important of all, relax and enjoy yourself. Check that you have a clean handkerchief – you would be surprised how emotional your wedding can be. Often it is the groom rather than the bride who is suddenly overcome by the emotion of the moment and is moved to shed tears. Remember too to take your speech notes and your small notebook and pen or pencil.

The best man will probably need a lift back once he has taken the car in which you will leave on honeymoon to the reception location. You might also cast your eye down the best man's list above, to check that he hasn't missed anything out. More importantly, try to ensure that you have not forgotten anything. Cufflinks? Buttonhole? Umbrella? If you find later that you have, don't worry. A member of the congregation will almost certainly be happy to supply the deficiency if the best man can't.

USHERS

Ushers should be at the church before anyone else and with time in hand to examine the layout and find the service sheets – forty-five minutes is usually sufficient. If the best man or groom has not already allocated areas of responsibility, the ushers should do this between themselves. The one who knows the bride's family best should obviously be in charge of the seating in the front pews on her side of the church (the left-hand half), according to the seating plan. A member of the groom's family should do the same for his side. One or two ushers stand by the door to greet guests and hand out service sheets, while the others answer questions and show people to suitable seats, walking with them all or some of the way (depending on the backlog of guests waiting to seat themselves at that moment) before returning to the church door. During the service the ushers sit in a pew reserved for them near the door. One should wait near the closed door during the first part of the service to open it for latecomers. After the service they linger near the best man in case he needs to ask them to give anyone a lift to the reception.

GUESTS

The question of what should be worn at a wedding sometimes causes great upheaval and confusion. In fact, the answer is very simple. Guests of both sexes take their lead from your parents. If your father is going to wear morning dress (black cut-away tailcoat with striped trousers), your fiancé and his best man should be similarly dressed, and so should male guests. Grey morning dress is also correct but looks smarter at weddings in spring and summer than in autumn and winter. Your mother will wear a smart short dress, coat and dress, or suit, with a matching hat. Her bag and shoes will match each other and possibly her hat. This is the usual form of dress for men and women at weddings for which a formal invitation has been issued and unless informed otherwise your guests should automatically dress in this manner.

If you want the men in particular to know that a more casual form of dress is acceptable – smart dark suits for example – this should be done by word of mouth rather than anything printed on the invitation. If the wedding is taking place late in the afternoon and will be followed by a dance, dress could be black tie rather than morning coats. This too is communicated by word of mouth rather than on the invitation. Alternatively, you could enclose a photocopied note with the invitations explaining that dress for the wedding is black tie and evening dresses. In this case the women don't have to wear hats.

If your fiancé is being married in uniform, his best man should also wear his (if he too is in the services), but the best man cannot wear uniform if the groom does not. In Scotland, dress kilts are the equivalent of morning dress elsewhere. Those not from Scotland should wear the usual morning dress. It is not considered correct to wear kilts at weddings outside Scotland. If there is a Scottish connection, however, pageboys could wear them, and tartan is attractive for winter bridesmaids.

Top hats used to be worn automatically with morning dress but have now all but been abandoned. Few men feel really comfortable wearing them, and they can look positively silly and affected if perched on the back of the head. If they are worn, the brims should be parallel with the ground. Men should remove their hats when entering a church (but in a synagogue heads should be covered). Women traditionally wear hats to a formal wedding, and these

should be worn for the reception following. If a guest has a hat that is too small and is uncomfortable she can remove it for the party, but in general the opportunity to dress up smartly is welcomed with enthusiasm, by male and female guests alike.

Some people hold that since this is the bride's day, no one else should dress in white or cream, and this does seem a sensible rule to follow as a matter of courtesy. Coloured shoes, bag and hat worn with white or cream, however, will prevent them looking 'bridal'. Because a wedding is a celebration, bright colours and patterns are appropriate, while black, dark grey and other deep and sombre shades are less so, unless they are relieved by splashes of bright colour or the wearer is in mourning.

All these 'rules' can be broken, of course. They simply provide a framework within which everyone knows what is what.

DISTINGUISHED GUESTS

Distinguished or honoured guests are people who are not members of the so-called 'bridal party' (consisting of you and your fiancé, your and his natural or adopted parents, best man and attendants) but who are more involved than other guests. The most usual are stepparents, who sit in the body of the church and amongst other guests at the reception, rather than in the front pews and at the high table. Your natural parent's current partner can be considered either as a distinguished guest or as a guest like any other, depending upon family attitudes and assuming you have invited them at all (which you should if you can as a kindness to your parent). Feathers can easily be ruffled in complicated family situations, and the allocation of 'distinguished guest' status can help smooth these over.

Other guests who are special are the person who is making the first speech and toast, your best friend (if she has declined to be a bridesmaid but has been closely involved in preparations) elderly relatives and visitors who have travelled from abroad especially to be at your wedding. You could allocate them specific seats near the front pews in church to ensure that they can see and hear well and place them at the head of a table at the meal afterwards, if there is one. In addition, a friend or relative could be appointed to take special care of each distinguished guest, escorting them in church and at the reception, making sure that they have refreshments and introducing them to your family and friends.

CHILDREN

You will have to decide on your policy regarding children before the guest list is finalised and the invitations sent out. If one of you has children, they should be as closely involved as possible in your wedding and should certainly be welcomed at the register office and place of worship. You may also be at that age when most of your friends seem to have children and there will a crowd of them at your reception, in which case you might consider engaging a children's entertainer to amuse them in a separate room, especially while the cake is being cut and speeches made. Various alternative plans of action are available to you (see right).

CHILDREN

1 = considerations   2 = provisions   3 = invitation

Children and babies are welcome at the church and at the reception or party following

1 Be prepared for noise in church, however good the children are usually. The formality of the situation may be a strain on them even if they are used to going to church services. Remember the video or sound recording and take the minister's views into account
2 Brief ushers about roughly how many families with children are expected and ask them to place them in pews where they can leave quietly during the service if necessary
3 Add Christian names only of small children and babies: Mr and Mrs Harry Fraser, Flora and William

The only small children in church will be your attendants; other children are welcome at the reception only

1 The parents of small children who are not attendants may not like the discrimination being made
2 Provide a crèche at a nearby building such as your parents' home or the village hall, with a registered childminder or nurse equipped with books, toys, biscuits and squash, etc. If it is a public building check safety, heating, loos, availability of kettle and mugs, etc.

3 Do not add children's names to the invitations but enclose a note saying they are welcome to the reception and firmly explaining the arrangements you have made for the service

No small children in church (your attendants are older children or adults); all children welcome at the reception

1 If the serenity of the religious service is important to you this is the ideal arrangement
2 As for previous point
3 As for previous point

No small children welcome either in church or at the reception

1 This is a rather unfriendly policy for what is, after all, a family occasion. Likely to be unpopular with some parents, especially those who live a long distance away and will have to make complicated childcare arrangements.
2 None. Be prepared for some parents to ring up and ask to bring their children, however, and if you are determined to exclude children altogether you will have to be stern and not give into pleading of special cases
3 Do not add children's names to invitations

SEATING IN THE CHURCH

The groom and his family and friends traditionally occupy the half of the church to the right of the central aisle as you face the altar, and the bride's family the left-hand half. The origin of this is the groom's assumed right-handedness. If he is right-handed, he needs that arm free to draw his sword or otherwise defend his bride and himself from marauding aggressors in church. She therefore stands to his left with her friends and relations ranked behind her, while his are positioned behind him. Today the tradition continues, even if the groom is left-handed and no marauders are anticipated.

The church may have more seats in one half than the other, where, for example, there is a lady chapel to the right of the nave, and there may have been more refusals from one family than the other. If as a result it is clear that one side of the church is becoming fuller than the other, ushers should invite guests to sit in the emptier half, regardless of allegiance. It is also quite likely that some guests when asked 'Bride or groom?' by the ushers, will reply 'Both!'. In this case they should be seated in the emptier side. Both sides are usually equally full by the time the bride arrives.

FRONT PEWS

A certain number of pews on each side of the church will be reserved for immediate family, the exact number depending on your interpretation of 'immediate'. Brothers, sisters, aunts and uncles, grandparents, godparents, and all their spouses and children can easily add up to eight or ten pews. There is absolutely nothing wrong with allocating specific seats for all these people. On the contrary, this is the only way of ensuring they have a ringside view. It is important, however, to be realistic about the number of seats in each pew and the number of pews needed. Don't try to squash an uncomfortable number into each pew.

One advantage of quite an extensive seating plan for the front pews is that it can include visitors from abroad (it would be a shame if they travelled so far only to sit

---

PREPARING THE CHURCH

In order for the church to be comfortable for your guests, check the following points:

▶ Who puts the heating on and how long before the guests arrive? Is it possible to increase the time or the temperature in case of particularly inclement weather?

▶ Does the church have a special carpet which is laid up the aisle for weddings? If so, arrange for this to be done well in advance of the first guests' arrival

▶ The church is probably kept spotlessly clean but, if you are worried, you or someone else could take a duster and have a quick check around on the morning of your wedding or the day before

---

right at the back) and other distinguished guests such as stepparents, without putting them before members of your family. Remind your fiancé to leave room on his seating plan for himself and his best man to sit in the front pew before the service. Alternatively, arrange for two chairs to be placed in front of the pews on their side. Also consider the bridesmaids – are they going to stand throughout the service or sit in a pew at the front?

If there are choir stalls at the front of the church, but no choir present at your marriage service, your and your fiancé's immediate family could sit there. This has several advantages. They will be able to see you clearly from the front rather than the back, the front pews will be free for other close family and friends which will allow for a little more seating space throughout the church. Consult the minister before deciding to use the choir stalls in this way.

Once the seating plan has been drawn up copies should be passed to the best man for the ushers. You can either leave it at that or prepare individual place cards and attach these to the pews in church.

SPECIAL SEATS

There may be guests who are not allocated places on the seating plan but to whose needs ushers need to be especially sensitive. If you have friends who will be bringing their babies or young children to church, they clearly need to be at the end of their pews and somewhere near the door so that they can, if necessary, take a child out quickly and relatively quietly. Elderly or disabled guests may wish to be similarly seated. If a guest has a wheelchair, find out from the minister in advance where he or she would be best placed, both for their own benefit and for the safety and convenience of others. The bride's route to the altar must be left clear. Ideally ushers should be briefed as to roughly how many families and frail, elderly people they should expect.

If any of your attendants are small children, you might think about where their parents should sit. Imagine what the experience of being your attendant must be like for a child – exciting but very strange and probably rather alarming. They can see rows and rows of (to them) huge grown-ups dressed rather grandly, and they too are dressed in unusual clothes and shoes. Their surroundings are impressive and unfamiliar. If they can turn their head and have the reassuring sight of their parents nearby they are more likely to cope with the experience. They are more likely to behave, and if they don't, their parents are on hand to restrain or comfort them. When tears are near, parents could perhaps dispense fruit pastilles to calm the nerves (not messy chocolate and not sweets with noisy wrappers). All in all, it's a good idea to include the children's parents on the seating plan, placing them as near the front as possible, at the pew end nearest the aisle and their children.

The marriage service joins you and your fiancé together into a single unit, a new family. It is an intensely personal matter, but also a public one, witnessed by relations and friends who represent the community in which you will live thereafter. The surroundings in which the service takes place are dignified and imposing, in keeping with the seriousness of the commitment you each make on your wedding day.

THE SERVICE

This is it. The day in which you have invested so much, emotionally and financially, and towards which you have been working for so long has finally arrived. Your life will never be the same again. You and your fiancé made your personal commitment to each other long ago, when you became engaged to be married. Now you are going to make that commitment in public, in front of the person who marries you, your witnesses, and a congregation of relatives and friends. If you have religious convictions and are being married in a religious service you are also making your vows in the presence of a higher being. Altogether, it is a pretty intense experience. All eyes are on you, but at the heart of the celebrations is the marriage ceremony itself.

It would take a huge volume to explore the possibilities of the marriage service in all its forms in every denomination and religion. The majority of weddings which take place in Britain in a place of worship are Church of England marriages, and many other Christian weddings follow very similar lines. It is that form of service that is discussed here (see pages 79–81 for details of Jewish and Greek Orthodox wedding ceremonies). The service starts with your arrival at church, but it is usual for the organist to play for 20 minutes or so beforehand, while guests are taking their seats. Ideas for this and all music for the service are included in the special section on music (see pages 73–75 for further details).

You have travelled from your or your parents' home with your father or the person who is giving you away. Your bridesmaids are waiting for you in the church porch and, once they have made sure that your dress and veil are in order, they line up behind you, the youngest first and oldest and tallest last. The person giving you away tucks your left arm into his right arm while the verger gives the organist a signal. There is a pause before organ music swells and thunders through the church, announcing your arrival. Everyone stands, and you are off, up the aisle between crowds of smiling faces, towards the altar, your husband and a new life.

If your father cannot give you away, the two parts of the traditional 'father's duties' can be divided. A male relative can escort you up the aisle to where your mother is waiting to give you away. After your father, your mother is the most appropriate person to 'give you' to your husband. The idea that it must be a man who gives you away is entrenched but unfounded; equally there is no reason why your mother cannot walk you up the aisle although this is rarely done. The alternative is for a relative, usually but not necessarily male, both to escort you up the aisle and to take a father's role in the service. This could be a grandfather, brother or uncle.

Sometimes family difficulties arise when the bride is closer to her stepfather than her natural father. These can be resolved by each man playing an important but different part in the day's events. One

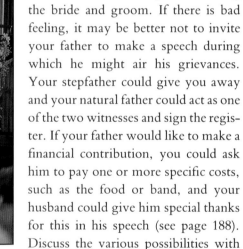

could give you away in church and the other make the first speech, toasting the bride and groom. If there is bad feeling, it may be better not to invite your father to make a speech during which he might air his grievances. Your stepfather could give you away and your natural father could act as one of the two witnesses and sign the register. If your father would like to make a financial contribution, you could ask him to pay one or more specific costs, such as the food or band, and your husband could give him special thanks for this in his speech (see page 188). Discuss the various possibilities with your fiancé. He knows the people involved but isn't emotionally involved himself, so may be able to give you objective advice, and he will of course give you complete support on the day. Whatever you decide, explain firmly and gently to your father, perhaps at a private meal with you and your fiancé.

As you walk up the aisle, the minister may walk in front of you, and possibly the choir in front of him, with a person carrying a cross at the very front of the procession. Ask the minister what the usual routine is in his church at the rehearsal so that you don't get a surprise on the day. When the music begins (this might be either a hymn or a piece of organ music) your fiancé and his best man step out from the front right-hand pew and stand at the chancel steps. The minister faces you on the steps. There is no need to hurry towards him. Take plenty of time, savouring your last moments with your father and concentrating on the ceremony to come. You will hardly notice the congregation. When you reach the chancel steps, turn and give your flowers to a bridesmaid (you will have decided which at the rehearsal) or place them on a previously arranged hassock. You need both hands free for your service sheet and the giving of hands and rings.

If the entrance music was not a hymn, one may be sung at this point. Here is an example of an order of service with three hymns, a psalm and one set of readings:

At the entrance of the Bride: organ music
Hymn: 'Praise, my soul, the King of heaven!'
The Marriage
The Responses
Psalm 121: 'I will lift up mine eyes unto the hills'
Reading: The Gospel according to St Mark 10: 6-9
Reading: 'Let me not to the marriage of true minds'
(Sonnet by William Shakespeare)
The Address
Hymn: 'Who would true valour see'
Prayers
The Lord's Prayer
Hymn: 'Ye holy Angels bright'
The Blessing
Signing the Register, during which music
is played in the body of the church
The Recession

Whenever you decide to have the first hymn, you will need a service sheet to read the words. Either the minister or the best man should have a copy each for you and your fiancé which he will hand you at this point, as well as having one for himself. Sort this out at the rehearsal. During the marriage itself you need to give back your service sheets in order to have your hands free, and you need them back again for the rest of the service.

Early in your discussions with your minister he will probably have asked you which form of the marriage service you would like. You may immediately think of the beautiful language of the older service, which asks: 'Wilt thou have this Man to thy wedded husband, to live together after God's ordinance in the holy estate of Matrimony?' It is poetic and historic, but the language of the modern service is beautiful too, in a different way. It is clear and direct, and many people have found its simplicity moving. There is another interesting and important difference between the two.

Each service gives three reasons for marriage: children, sex and friendship. The 1966 service (based on the 1662 Book of Common Prayer) puts them in that order, with 'the procreation of children' as the first and most important. Sex comes second, so that 'such persons as have not the gift of continence' may none the less continue to be members of the church, not celibate but not sinning. Friendship, or 'mutual society, help and comfort' comes third and last. The 1977 service reverses this order, putting friendship first, sex second and children third. This is the logical order for the modern world. After all, not every couple is lucky enough to be able to have children, which the older service claims is the primary reason for marriage. And few marriages *not* based on the mutual liking and respect which is the first requirement of friendship are likely to last or be happy.

With the modern service you and you fiancé can choose whether or not to say that he will worship you and you will obey him. 'Worship' and 'obey' go hand-in-hand in the service – you either have both or neither – so that there is a mutual obligation, not simply an undertaking on your part to do what you are told. With the older version of the service you can simply choose to omit the reference to obeying your husband.

The modern version of the service shows that the Church of England is moving forward in its thinking and by using it you will be supporting that move. If you find some of the wording a little too blunt it is possible to incorporate phrases from the old service at one or two important points, with the agreement of your minister. The responses may be one of these, where you may feel that the older service has greater depth and poetry than the plain wording of the newer.

During the last part of the marriage service you and your fiancé kneel. Hassocks for you both, or a wedding kneeler if the church has one, will either have been positioned by the verger before the service or should be moved into place at the appropriate time by the best man. This should be sorted out at the rehearsal.

In the early planning of your wedding service you may find you have so many ideas for the music, psalms, hymns and readings that you are in danger of turning the event into a three-hour recital. Three quarters of an hour to an hour is ample for a wedding service. If it is much longer the most important part of it, your marriage, is in danger of being buried. Try to balance performed music, hymns which enable the congregation to join in and contribute to a joyful communal sound, and readings which express your personal feelings about what you are undertaking.

Readings are usually from the Bible. The prayer book contains a list of suggestions and your minister will also have ideas about appropriate passages from the Old and New Testaments. If your minister agrees to the idea, you could in addition have readings such as a poem found in an anthology of love poetry or a passage from a philosophical work. The sonnet by Elizabeth Barrett Browning that begins 'How do I love thee? Let me count the ways' is a popular choice. The British Humanist Association (see page 82) produces a booklet called *To Love and to Cherish* which suggests some beautiful non-religious readings.

Your minister will almost certainly want to see your proposed readings before he gives his consent to anything not drawn from the Bible, and it would be courteous to check that he approves even Bible passages before making the final decision.

The address is a form of sermon, in which the minister 'addresses' some thoughts about marriage in general and about your marriage in particular, to you and to the assembled congregation. It isn't absolutely necessary to have an address, and if your minister is notorious for being inaudible or for droning on for far too long on Sundays, it might be as well to try to persuade him that no address is necessary. You could suggest that he gives you a personal address the previous evening, before the rehearsal (or afterwards), as you don't think you will take much in during the marriage ceremony itself. If he is a good preacher, however, the address may turn out to be one of the highlights of the service.

During the readings and address you and your husband can either remain standing or sit down. You may think it is a long time to stand, but in fact the time goes in a flash and you shouldn't find that you become uncomfortable. If in doubt, arrange for chairs or stools to be placed on one side before the service. On the left of the aisle below the pulpit is a good place, where they are not in the way of the best man and the lectern. You either move to the chairs and sit or they can be moved into the middle where you have been standing. Furniture removal in the middle of the service is generally not a good idea, however. It creates noise and disruption, and your dress may become entangled, so it is better to go to the chairs rather than bringing them to you.

During the hymn which follows the address the minister will lead you and your husband to the altar step for the prayers. He stands to speak the prayers while you and the congregation kneel. The prayer book contains many prayers suitable for the marriage service which refer to love, marriage, children and family life. Prayers on these and other subjects can also be found in other books which your minister may be able to lend you or you may find in the library. Or you can adapt existing prayers or write your own on a related subject which is important to you. Submit your choice and your compositions to the minister, leaving plenty of time for discussion and revision if necessary. The Blessing is another form of prayer, spoken by the minister just before the signing of the register. It rounds off the marriage with a request for blessing not only upon you both but upon the whole congregation who have witnessed your vows and taken part in the service. Once it has been spoken the minister will lead the way into the vestry for the signing of the register.

This is the end of the religious service. Signing the register completes the civil requirements for your marriage to be valid. Once the music which you have arranged for the entertainment of the congregation has been performed, you and your husband process out of the church followed by your attendants, parents, family and friends.

The minister who marries you may customarily give the blessing after the signing of the register, so that it is the final word in the service. This makes sense in theory but in practice it creates an awkward hiatus which your minister may not be aware of. The bride and groom and their entourage emerge from the vestry and have to hang around in front of the altar while the blessing is pronounced. If possible, persuade him that you want the blessing beforehand so that it rounds off the religious part of the service, keeping the secular signing ceremony completely separate. He may, of course, wish to stick with tradition in which case you will have to acquiesce.

SIGNING AND LEAVING

THE PROCESSION INTO THE VESTRY

Most vestries are quite small, so the only people who follow you there after the prayers are the best man, your attendants and both .pairs of natural or adopted parents. Stepparents and friends do not join the vestry party, unless you have previously arranged that they will be witnesses and sign the register, but this is unusual. The photographer usually follows, to record the moment, and then quietly leaves by an outside door in order to be ready when you and your husband emerge from the church. If you are wearing a veil you can lift it back from your face when you arrive in the vestry, which will make it easier to sign the register.

Once the last person has disappeared into the vestry, the congregation is usually treated to a recital of music played by the organist, perhaps with an instrumental soloist, and possibly sung by the choir or a soloist.

WHO SIGNS THE REGISTER

Signing the register completes the civil requirements of the marriage service and ensures you are married in the eyes of the law as well as according to the rites of your religion and denomination. All incumbents in the Church of England are licensed to register marriages they have conducted, and the ministers in a large proportion of places of worship outside the Church of England are also qualified to act as registrar for marriages. In some denominations or places of worship the celebrant is not qualified, or the building is not licensed, and it will be necessary for you to have a separate, civil marriage in a register office before you are legally married.

The correct page of the register will previously have been completed by the incumbent, so that it only requires the necessary signatures for the documentation to be complete. Five signatures are required:

1 You sign in your maiden name
2 Your husband signs
3 and 4 Two witnesses sign. By custom these are usually one of your parents and one of your husband's parents, but any adult who has been present can act as witness and sign the register
5 The officiant signs

Once the formalities are completed, which only takes a few moments, there is usually much kissing and exchanging of congratulations.

It's an exciting moment. You are now well and truly married in the eyes of both Church and State.

On a more practical level, if you need to adjust your veil or any other element of your appearance, this is the moment to do so. When you can hear that the music being played in the body of the church has come to an end, you all line up (see below) ready for the recession and await the minister's signal to proceed.

THE RECESSION

Traditionally when the time came for the procession to form at the end of the service, the best man stayed behind to pay the fees and tip the verger. This can be arranged in advance with the minister, however, so that the best man generally joins the recession. The usual order is as follows:

ALTAR

Bride's father　Groom's mother
Groom's father　Bride's mother
Best man　Chief bridesmaid
Small bridesmaids and pages
Groom　Bride

DOOR

When you emerge from the vestry, you may be in for a shock. For the first time you will see and notice the mass of people who have been present all through your marriage service, but of whom you have hardly been aware. During the ceremony you do not turn to face them. Such is the intimacy of the marriage itself that you almost feel as if you are in a small room with the minister, your father, your husband and the best man. Your first face-on sight of the congregation brings home to you the realisation of what has just happened. You and your husband came to church as individuals, but you are leaving as a married couple. It will take some time for the fact that you are now married to sink in, possibly for the rest of your life, starting with this moment.

MUSIC IN CHURCH

Music can add an extra dimension to a marriage service. Besides being spiritually uplifting, it gives everyone present the chance to join in. Before you arrive at the church, the organ's quiet playing adds to the air of anticipation and excitement as your family and friends await your entrance. Then when you actually arrive, your progress up the aisle is helped along by a stately and dignified piece of music.

Rousing hymns bring everyone together in joyful celebration, while psalms are more thoughtful and the tempo of the music will reflect this. The signing of the register gives the opportunity for the congregation to enjoy a musical interlude. And, finally, there is the triumphant moment when you appear before the assembled crowd as a married couple and make your exit from the church, at which point the music fills the church with the glory of the moment. As you emerge from the church, a peal of bells fills the air.

For the non-musician, that can seem a lot of music to find and choose. Where do you begin? You have heard music at your friends' weddings, but you don't simply want to recycle the same old tunes. How do you set about finding the organ music and the hymns and music for the signing of the register, that is exactly right for you and your wedding? It can seem a daunting task.

Start with your resident professionals. Your minister, organist and choir leader will probably have performed countless weddings and be a fund of helpful suggestions. The organist can give you a demonstration of the organ's abilities and at the same time play you various possible pieces for different parts of the service. If he or she, or the organ demonstrate that they are not really up to the task, you will have to think in terms of simple pieces he or she *can* play or that will sound good on the instrument. If instead you decide to find a professional organist from elsewhere (ask at your local reference library or music college), handle the situation with tact as you don't want to offend the resident organist. Alternatively, you may like to have a friend or relation playing at your wedding (with the minister's permission). He or she can add a special personal touch to your wedding and the resident organist, however good he or she is, should be understanding.

If you are not already a member, join your local music library and

Music is the natural expression of joy and hope for the future and throughout history it has been linked with church celebrations.

borrow some tapes or records. Don't only select original organ music. Many pieces initially written for other instruments have been adapted for the organ – a knowledgeable librarian will guide your research.

In some very small or old churches there is no organ, in which case you will need to hire musicians to play and lead the congregation. Their instruments need to be heard over the congregation's singing – brass or other wind instruments are ideal. If you have some ideas for music, discuss these with the musicians or ensemble to whom you speak about the possibility of playing at your wedding. Otherwise, make it clear that you need some guidance as to what they should play and that the final choice of music is important to you.

Don't dismiss the music you hear at other people's weddings. The reason certain pieces of music appear over and over again at weddings is that they are especially beautiful and appropriate, and in some cases like Wagner's Bridal Chorus from *Lohengrin* (popularly known as 'Here comes the bride') and Mendelssohn's 'Wedding March' from *Midsummer Night's Dream*, they have specific wedding associations. Other pieces of music exactly capture the mood for a particular moment in the service, like Widor's exciting 'Toccata' from the Fifth Symphony for the exit of bride and groom. If you have kept the service sheets from friends's weddings use them as a source of ideas.

Give a thought to the length of the aisle when choosing a piece of music for your procession. Pace it out while you are with the organist or use a tape of the music you are considering. You don't want to have to scurry to the altar, but you don't want to be stranded there either. You need just a few minutes at the chancel steps in which to settle and make sure everything is in order and everyone in their place.

Two, three or four hymns are all quite usual, but if you also have a psalm, two or three are sufficient. In general, people are less familiar with psalms than hymns and need a strong choir to lead them. Unless you have full confidence in your local choir you could consider having a fourth hymn instead of a psalm. Some psalms, like Psalm 23, 'The Lord is my Shepherd', have been adapted to hymn tunes. If you do have a psalm, choose a traditional chant and ask the choir to sing both that and the hymns in unison rather than parts, in order to give the congregation a good firm lead.

It is best to choose hymn tunes which everyone will know rather than little-known masterpieces that the congregation will have great difficulty following. Check that the organist will play each hymn in a sensible key – not too high or low – so that everyone can join in comfortably. And check the tunes themselves with the organist; some hymns can be sung to more than one tune and you don't want to hear the wrong one in the middle of your marriage service.

As well as the best-known traditional hymns, consider ones with personal associations, such as your or your fiancé's old school hymn, or 'Eternal Father, strong to save' ('For those in peril on the sea') if one of you has a seafaring connection. You could also use modern words to a familiar tune.

It does not usually take more than a few minutes for everyone concerned to sign the register and by this stage, when the service is almost over, the congregation may become impatient if the musical interlude goes on for too long, however beautiful it is. You generally have the choice of organ music, organ accompanying a singer or singers (the resident choir, for example), or organ with other instruments or a sung anthem. Wind instruments go well with the organ, and in particular the flute is popular. Songs whose words

reflect the joy of the occasion are appropriate too – the words could appear in the service sheet if there is room. The choir leader will probably be able to make some suggestions for suitable pieces. Whatever your final choice, ensure that it is fairly rigorous and loud or the congregation may become restless and talk. Quiet, subdued organ music, however exquisite, can be drowned by the excited chatter of friends and relations who may not have seen each other for months or years.

The music that announces to the world that the marriage is complete, and that your new life is beginning, needs to be magnificent – loud and bright, filling every corner of the church. It should also, ideally, last until the entire congregation has left the church. Once outside, they should be greeted by the ringing of the church bells, an incomparable sound. Sadly, many churches no longer have bells, or only have mechanical chimes which hardly compare for effect. If this is the case there is nothing to be done but ask the organist to keep playing until everyone has left. If his piece finishes too soon he can begin it again and keep going until the church is empty so that your guests have the joyful ring of organ music in their ears as they emerge into the open and make their way to the celebrations that follow.

RIGHT Veronica and Noel met at the church where she was a keen gospel singer, and the choir led gospel singing at their marriage. Human voices joined in songs of praise and joy are natural music for a wedding.

RIGHT Katrin and David were married surrounded by the mellow stone and majestic splendour of Milton Abbey in Dorset, where César Franck's duet *Panis Angelicus* seemed perfect for the occasion.

IDEAS FOR WEDDING MUSIC

THE ENTRANCE OF THE BRIDE

Arrival of the Queen of Sheba (Handel)
Bridal Chorus from *Lohengrin* (Wagner)
Introduction to Imperial March (Elgar)
Rondeau from Abdelazer (Purcell)
Trumpet Tune and Air (Purcell)
Trumpet Voluntary (Clarke)

SOME TRADITIONAL HYMNS

Dear Lord and Father of mankind
For the beauty of the earth
Guide me, O thou great Redeemer
Lead us, heavenly Father, lead us
'Lift up your hearts!'
Lord of all hopefulness
Love divine, all loves excelling
Praise to the Lord, the Almighty
Praise, my soul, the King of heaven
The King of love my shepherd is

ORGAN PIECES, ANTHEMS AND SONGS FOR THE SIGNING OF THE REGISTER

Allegro in G (Fiocco)
Aria from Suite in D (Air on a G string) (Bach)
Ave Maria (Schubert)
Be thou faithful unto Death (Mendelssohn)
Domine Deus (Vivaldi)
Hark, hark! the echoing air a triumph sings (After Shakespeare/Purcell)
Hornpipes and Scotch Tune from Amphitryon (Purcell)
I would be true (Anon – sung to the tune of 'the Londonderry Air', by Howard Walter)
Jesu, joy of man's desiring (Bach)
Largo from the 'New World' Symphony No. 9 in E minor (Dvořák)
Music for a Musical Clock (Haydn)

O come, O come, my dearest, and hither bring (Attrib. Pritchard/ Arne)
Panis Angelicus (Franck)
Sheep may safely graze (Bach)
Te Deum (Britten)
Wedding Cantata No. 22 (Bach)

PSALMS

The Lord is my shepherd (Psalm 23)
I will lift up mine eyes unto the hills (Psalm 121)

THE EXIT OF BRIDE AND GROOM

Allegro from Concerto No. 1 in G major (Bach)
Crown Imperial (Walton)
Fantasia in G minor (Bach)
Grand March from Aida (Verdi)
Hornpipe from the Water Music (Handel)
Toccata in D from Fifth Symphony (Widor)

It is traditional at Jewish weddings for the synagogue and in particular the huppah to be decorated with garlands of fresh flowers. Lauren and Michael are United Jews, observing Jewish customs less rigidly than Orthodox Jews but more strictly than Reformed Jews and Liberal Jews, and at their synagogue women sit on one side and men opposite them on the other. Clarke's Trumpet Voluntary greeted her as she arrived, accompanied by her brother Lloyd. Michael and other men present had their heads covered at all times and also wore traditional wedding clothes – morning coats – or black tie, as the marriage ceremony was followed by a dinner-dance at a large hotel. Marriage is considered the ideal state of being, ordained at the very moment of creation. The ceremony was once followed by seven days of feasting, now represented by the seven blessings sung before the cutting of the cake at the reception. After the blessings, which were sung at Lauren's wedding by three relations and close family friends, the bride and groom share the cup of wine used in the ceremony, as Lauren and Michael are shown doing here.

A JEWISH WEDDING

The Talmud, the primary source of Jewish religious law and tradition, says that a man is incomplete without a wife.

If you are Jewish and planning to get married then you probably know that the ceremony takes place under a square canopy whose four supporting poles are usually decorated with garlands of flowers. Known as the huppah (or chuppa, or chupa), the canopy is thought to hark back to biblical days when the Israelites were forced by circumstance to live in tents in the desert. The huppah is usually in a synagogue, but doesn't have to be: along with Quaker weddings, Jewish weddings are excluded from the laws which specify where and when you can be married. You can be married anywhere, at any time (except for the Sabbath, festival days and possibly certain other days), so long as you are married under a huppah.

On the day of the wedding, you and your fiancé will probably fast until after the marriage. As you arrive, wearing a traditional white gown, head-dress and veil and carrying flowers, sung psalms are followed by a chant of welcome. You stand under the canopy on your fiancé's right with your parents, and your bridesmaids stand nearby. Your fiancé is similarly supported by his parents, with his best man nearby, and all men present have their heads covered, perhaps by top hats.

The ceremony itself is in two parts, the first signifying your betrothal, the second your marriage. The betrothal establishes that you are able and willing to marry each other, rather as the banns do in the Anglican Church. During the betrothal, you and your fiancé each drink from a cup of wine which is handed by your mother to you and then by your fiancé's mother to him. You do not speak at any point in the proceedings, but your fiancé places your wedding ring on the forefinger of your right hand and says 'Behold, thou art consecrated unto me by this ring, according to the law of Moses and Israel'. You are now married in the eyes of Jewish law. Later

Lauren and Michael were married in London on a beautiful summer's day in July. Lauren wore a splendid white gown with a head-dress and veil – Jewish brides dress exactly as Christian ones do. They spent their first night at the hotel where their party was held and left the next day for an exotic honeymoon in the Far East.

you can transfer the ring to your left hand.

The marriage contract or ketubah, to which your husband has agreed before your arrival, is read and signed by you both and by two witnesses who must be unrelated to either of you and are usually the rabbi and cantor. It is then handed to you to keep. The ketubah contains the promises your husband makes to you on marriage; your consent to be bound by marriage is embodied in your acceptance of the ring.

Next, the seven blessings of marriage are pronounced. You and your husband each drink from the cup of wine which represents the cup of life in general and your new life together in particular. This time it is handed to you by your mother-in-law and then to your husband by your mother.

In the ceremony's most dramatic moment, your husband crushes a glass underfoot (usually safely wrapped in a napkin). There are various interpretations of this gesture. One is that it is a reminder of the destruction of the Temple in Jerusalem; another that the shattered glass symbolises the weakness of marriage without love; yet another that life inevitably holds misfortune as well as joy. The ceremony ends with a blessing, followed by the signing of the civil marriage register, after which you and your husband are led to a room where you remain alone together for a few minutes. This signals to the community that you are married and signifies the beginning of the consummation of your marriage. You may both break your fast here. Afterwards you join your family and friends in joyful festivities, with food, drink, speeches, blessings and often songs and dancing.

Moulla and John first met when they were
hardly more than babies; 22 years later they
were married in London with all the
traditional Greek Cypriot customs. Just
before leaving for the church Moulla,
serenaded by a violinist, was blessed by her
parents with a red scarf – a symbol of good
luck. When she arrived at church with her
father, John was ready to present her with her
bouquet. Her head-dress was made of silk
flowers and tiny pearls which also cascaded in
strings from the back. The crowns used for
the Service of the Crowns were similar and
fitted well with Moulla's head-dress. After
the marriage ceremony, a reception and dance
were held at a large hotel, and after dinner
Moulla and John performed a traditional
wedding dance. Later, guests pinned money
on their clothes – a Greek tradition intended
to help a newly married couple buy and equip
their new home together.

A GREEK ORTHODOX WEDDING

In the Greek Orthodox church, mass is celebrated on Sunday mornings, usually followed by christenings, with wedding taking place in the early- and mid-afternoons. When you arrive at church, your fiancé is waiting at the door to greet you and present you with your bouquet. The priest then leads the wedding procession to the soleas, the area in front of the altar screen where your marriage ceremony will take place. Behind him is your fiancé and his father; you walk behind them, veiled and holding your father's right arm, followed by your attendants. At the soleas you stand on your fiancé's left, facing the icon of the Virgin Mary on the altar screen whilst he faces the icon of Christ.

In front of you is the soleas table where the ceremonial bible, a dish of sugared almonds, a chalice of wine, a tray holding your rings, and the ceremonial crowns have been placed in preparation for your wedding. A child stands on each side of the table holding a large, decorated wedding candle, symbolising a wish for your lives to be bright and full like the flame and a prayer that your sins may be melted away as the wax melts. Your parents are behind them to the left, your fiancé's to the right.

The first part of the marriage ceremony is known as the Service of the Rings. After it comes the Service of the Crowns. The priest opens the first of these services from behind the table, intoning prayers for the church, for peace and a special prayer for your rings. Then, he moves forward and places the wedding rings on the fourth finger of your and your fiancé's right

hands. Traditionally, the best man then comes forward and swaps them back and forth three times. Today, when your fiancé is likely to have many supporters, rather than just one best man, each supporter (and indeed each of your bridesmaids) takes it in turn to swap the rings from you and your fiancé's hands, being careful to finish with the correct ring on each hand.

The Service of the Crowns now begins, with the priest again intoning three lengthy prayers, during the third of which he joins your right hands, which stay held together until the end of the ceremony. He then lifts the crowns from the table and holds them over your heads with his arms crossed and makes three blessings, uncrossing and re-crossing his arms after each. Made from wax pearls, sparkling diamante or lace and joined to each other by a ribbon, the crowns symbolise the glory and honour bestowed on you and your new marriage by the church as well as signifying that in your home you will be queen and king.

Once the priest has completed his blessings, the crowns are handed to the best man, who stands behind you and repeats the ritual of exchanging them between blessings. Then the wedding lessons are read: the fifth chapter of the letter of St Paul to the Ephesians, and the second chapter of St John's Gospel (referring to the miracle of changing water into wine at the marriage at Cana). This is followed by the Lord's Prayer, which you and the congregation join together to speak. This is the only point at which anyone other than the priest, deacon and cantor or choir speak or sing; you and your fiancé will have given your consent and made your undertakings

when signing documents some time before the wedding.

The priest blesses the chalice of wine, known as the 'common cup', from which you each drink three times. The cup of wine is a reminder of the sorrows and joys you will experience and share. The priest then guides you in a stately procession three times around the table. As you walk, he chants the hymn of St John Damaskinos as a signal that the sacrament of marriage is complete and that you are welcomed into the Christian community as a married couple.

The marriage ceremony closes with more prayers, before the priest takes the bible and with it strikes your hands apart. Your relatives now gather round informally to offer congratulations, kiss the bible, you and your husband, and the crowns. The festivities follow with feasting and dancing, and the sugared almonds are distributed amongst the unmarried girls and women. Blessed in a marriage service, a sugared almond is believed to help a girl find her husband, and if she sleeps with it under her pillow she may even dream of him.

There are three ways of fulfilling the civil requirements of marriage in conjunction with a Greek Orthodox wedding. Frequently, a couple is married in a register office ceremony the previous day or some days before. In some circumstances it is possible to sign the register in the church, immediately after the religious marriage. The third alternative is to incorporate the civil undertakings into the religious service, but this is unusual. Your priest will guide you as to what is possible and permissible.

REGISTER OFFICE WEDDING

THE CEREMONY

The civil marriage ceremony is short and to the point. As with any legal marriage, you and your fiancé make a declaration and a contract. You each declare in front of two witnesses that you are free to marry, and then you each state that you are taking the other as your husband/wife. That is all that is required by law, and the ceremony is determinedly secular. It takes about ten minutes, and it is not necessary for there to be a wedding ring or rings.

Before the marriage takes place you and your wedding party may have to wait for a few minutes in a waiting room at the register office. Then an official will ask the two of you alone to join him to check the documentation and ask if you intend to use a ring or rings. If you do, he includes the giving of the ring or the exchange of rings in the ceremony at an appropriate point (exactly when is left to his discretion). Once he is satisfied that the legal preparations are in order, the witnesses and any guests are invited to join you (or the three of you go back to join them) and the ceremony takes place.

The speed of the civil marriage ceremony and lack of any opportunity to give expression to your feelings of love and your beliefs about the seriousness of what you are undertaking, combined with the institutional surroundings, may leave some people who have chosen or found it necessary to have a civil marriage with a feeling that the job has not been properly done. Some sort of follow-up ceremony is sometimes needed to fulfil our natural desire for an event of such importance in our lives to be given a cultural context complete with familiar rituals. Civil marriage is also a relatively private business, conducted in municipal offices, whereas marriage as a social institution is a public affair and a follow-up ceremony can help to place it in the broader context of the community and in particular of our wider circle of family and friends. Such ceremonies are either religious or non-religious.

SERVICE OF BLESSING

The most familiar is the Church of England service of blessing whose official name is the Service of Prayer and Dedication. This is available at the discretion of your parish minister, under the guidance of his Diocesan Bishop, and, because it is his personal decision, he is likely to want to know in great detail the circumstances which

made a civil marriage necessary for you. If either of you is divorced he may ask about the reasons for the break-up and details of your or your fiancé's lifestyle since. It is only reasonable that he should satisfy himself that you are serious and sincere about wanting the Church's blessing, and you should co-operate with his enquiries. If you are a regular member of his congregation and you declare your intentions in terms of baptism and church membership for any children resulting from your marriage this may also influence him.

The length and content of the service are other matters which are left to the minister's discretion. A Church of England service of blessing can be brief and austere with only a few witnesses or it can include music, hymns, readings, and an address, and involve a large number of guests, much like a wedding. It is generally considered inappropriate, however, for the trappings to imitate an actual wedding. Although you can probably wear white and carry flowers, you should not wear a veil, for instance. The minister may also not consider it appropriate for you to have attendants, especially if you have been married before.

Other religions and denominations do or don't have the equivalent of a service of blessing according to their views on marriage and divorce. Some Protestant denominations, such as the Church of Scotland, may marry divorced people. The Roman Catholic Church does not recognise civil divorce except as a preliminary to an annulment of a marriage, but it does celebrate a Service of Convalidation which is a simplified form of the marriage service. This is available to couples who have had register-office weddings for reasons other than being legally divorced and having a previous spouse living. Convalidation usually takes place some considerable time after the wedding, sometimes ten or twenty years, and is generally a quiet, private affair. The Jewish faith, by contrast, has its own form of divorce, the *get*, which enables previously married people to be remarried in the synagogue. Your local religious leader should be able to explain the position held by your faith or denomination.

HUMANIST CEREMONY

It seems unreasonable that only those with religious affiliations have the opportunity to follow a civil marriage with a ceremony of celebration. Many people who do not believe in a 'God' have none the less strong views on moral issues and feel deeply that marriage is an event of sufficient personal and communal importance to deserve more than the civil ceremony gives. There is nothing to stop you holding a ceremony of readings and music during which you each read or speak some lines about your love for each other and your aspirations for your marriage. The British Humanist Association, 14 Lamb's Conduit Passage, London WC1R 4R11 (tel: 071 430 0908), will help you find someone to conduct your service of celebration. They also produce a booklet with suggestions for the celebration format as well as examples of suitable music and read-ings. In their experience, some university chaplains and Unitarian ministers are prepared to perform a non-religious marriage cere-mony in a building licensed for marriage and incorporating the declaration and contract which make a marriage legally binding. Under these circumstances it would not be necessary to have a separate civil wedding. Your marriage certificate will indicate the denomination of the building in which you were married.

New legislation is planned which will allow secular civil mar-riages to take place at licensed buildings other than places of worship and register offices. Enquire at your register office for details.

SUMMER GLORY

Caroline and Nick met in Norwich, a stone's throw from the cathedral where they were to be married. For their wedding, Caroline wore a specially-designed dress of ivory silk. Its soft boat neck, billowing puff sleeves and nipped-in waist perfectly suited her slender figure. She wore her hair in its usual well-cut style, and her head-dress was a mixture of silk flowers and fresh gypsophila. Seven bridesmaids wore peach taffeta dresses from Liberty and two pageboys wore ivory. Each little boy had a big bow at his neck, a straw boater on his head and a teddy bear in his hand (the tiny bridesmaids had one each too). Caroline and her father and attendants strolled from her parents' home to the neighbouring cathedral for her marriage to Nick, and afterwards excited friends and relations greeted them in the magnificent cloister. Then a 1930 Bentley whisked them off to the reception and the cutting of a towering four-tier cake.

WINTER MAGIC

Annelise and Mark were married just before Christmas, on a blustery day warmed by the rich colours and fabrics which she chose for herself, her attendants, and even Mark's and the best man's waistcoats. Annelise is a dress designer and created her own wedding gown from gold-embroidered guipure lace with a deep, low shawl collar that stood away from and showed off her beautiful shoulders. The sleeves were unlined, revealing both the magnificence of the lace and the slimness of her arms. Her bridesmaids wore vibrant red silk tartan dresses with ivy-green sashes and shoes, while three pageboys were dressed in green taffeta knickerbockers, white lacy shirts and gold waistcoats. The Christmas theme was carried through the flowers and foliage – holly, ivy, mistletoe, fir and Christmas roses – to the cake. Three unfussy layers were each wreathed in swags of holly made from icing. Guests at the wedding were swept away by another original idea – a balloon-filled double-decker bus which took them from the church to the reception.

FAIRYTALE WEDDING

Ann and Guy's wedding made a child's fairytale come true. When she was a little girl, Ann treasured her Cinderella storybook and dreamt of having a dress just like Cinderella's ballgown for her wedding. When she and Guy decided to get married, she still had the book, and her wedding dress was indeed copied from it. Her mother is a professional dressmaker and created the gown from organza, embroidered with sequins and beads, laid over satin, with hoops and panniers to support its fullness. The pages wore Prince Charming outfits with brocaded Regency coats and frilly white shirts over buttoned britches. The wedding cake also had a fairytale element – a miniature fountain under a colonnade of white arches supporting three layers decorated with yellow icing flowers. Inside, it was rich and spicy, made from an old Grenadan recipe.

HISTORIC ROMANCE

Melissa and Morgan met at a regimental dance, but it was Melissa's work as a picture restorer in a national museum that prompted her to have a historically-inspired wedding dress. The research and construction involved every detail, starting with the petticoat. A fine hoop crinoline, it was made from watch spring steel, as in Victorian times, and the fullness of the sleeves was also maintained with hoops. The dress itself was ivory dupion silk and the embroidered panels were stitched by a beadwork expert. The inspiration for their design of intricate interlocking scrolls came from fourth-century Celtic scrolls discovered in the 1950s. Each panel was embroidered with gold thread, crystals and pearls on a heavy vilene fabric stretched on a quilting frame. The skirt was attached to the bodice with 434 hand-sewn cartridge pleats. In order to continue the Celtic theme, and so as not to detract from the elaborate detail of her dress, Melissa decided to restrain her hair, plaited and knotted, under a neat cap, from under which her veil fell in a soft cascade.

this, applied direct or with a small brush, before filling in with colour. Blot with tissue paper and add another layer. Choose drier rather than greasier lipstick, and ask your mother to keep your lipstick and powder in her handbag so you can check your face during the day.

Teeth

13 Pink and red lipstick make teeth look even whiter. If you have naturally white teeth, you will be able to wear browns and corals on your lips, but avoid these colours if your teeth tend to be yellow as they emphasise yellow tones. Have a dental check-up as soon as you become engaged – you don't want any painful surprises just before the wedding. Visit your dentist or dental hygienist for a professional clean a week before your wedding day.

Hands

14 Everyone will want to look at your rings, and during the service your hands are a focus of attention, so it is worth taking trouble to ensure they are soft, neat and clean. Use rubber gloves to do the washing-up. After washing your hands during the day, use a small amount of good-quality hand cream or moisturiser and remember to rub it into the backs of your hands as well as the palms and fingers. Avoid wearing rings other than your engagement ring in the weeks before your wedding as dirt and soap caught under the shank and mount can cause irritation and unsightly red patches between your fingers. For silky soft hands wash them about once a month with a facial scrub to remove dry skin.

Nails

15 Take special care of your nails in the months before your wedding, perhaps treating yourself to a regular manicure. Certainly have a manicure on the day or the day before you get married. Try giving yourself a manicure: wash your hands thoroughly in warm soapy water (don't soak them), dry, massage nail cream in and wait for three minutes. Ease cuticles away from nails, clean under the nails and then wash and dry. Buff and add a final rub of nail cream. Keep your nails trim and not too long – the longer and untidier the more likely you are to have a tear just when you least want it – and stick to colourless or very pale-tinted clear varnish. Brightly coloured talons are inappropriate on a bride.

Feet

16 You will be on your feet for most of your wedding day so they need to be supple and well rested. Put them up for as much of the previous day as you can, and get them into shape over the preceding weeks, soaking them, massaging them, removing hard skin and rubbing in softening cream. Visit a chiropodist well in advance for some toning exercises. If you normally wear low-heeled or flat shoes, wear the same for your wedding. High heels are much more tiring and can actually damage your feet. Whatever the shoes, ensure they fit properly.

Body skin

17 Bathtime is extra luxurious if you add mustard or milk powder to the water. Mustard is invigorating and supposed to ease stiff joints; milk makes you feel like Cleopatra and your skin feel silky smooth. Sea salt crystals added to the water will help draw out impurities.

Perspiration

18 If you are at all worried about perspiration, sew dress shields into the armpits of your dress – two in each sleeve if they will make you feel more confident. Mention this to your dressmaker or bear it in mind when buying your dress as the shields will make the tops of your sleeves tighter. Use a strong anti-perspirant: there are certain creams available or try an unscented man's anti-perspirant deodorant. Try anything new well in advance to ensure your skin doesn't have a reaction to an unfamiliar product. Avoid aerosol sprays.

Scent

19 You have three choices: a scent you regularly use and which you know suits you; a new sophisticated scent which you can have fun choosing; a fine floral scent which will continue the scent of your flowers. Whichever you choose, enjoy it, and avoid all other scented products. You want your scent to be clean and fresh, not muddied by a mixture of perfumed cosmetics, creams and bathtime preparations. If your chosen scent is available in various forms – bath oil, soap, moisturiser, body lotion, etc. – you can build up a rich but subtle scent by using these and topping them off with some eau-de-toilette or eau-de-parfum (longer lasting) behind your ears and on your wrists before you dress. Don't dress until your scent is dry – if it gets on your wedding clothes the oils may stain them.

Practice makes perfect

20 The key to confidence on your wedding day is practice. Leave yourself plenty of time (weeks and months, not days) to try out new effects and products, and when you discover what you like, practise and make the look your own. You may end up with the same routine you have always been happy with, which your fiancé and family know and like and which you know suits you. Or you may change the way you make up and no one will notice (the sign of subtlety) except to think that you look even more radiant than ever. Keep it simple and keep it honest to your real looks.

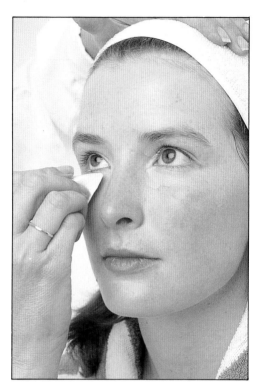

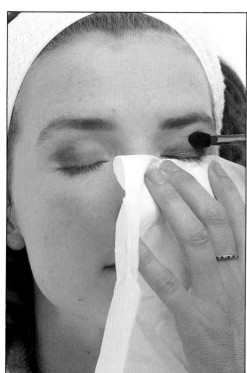

Practise your wedding make-up before the day of your marriage, especially if you plan to do anything different to your usual look. Natural-looking make-up is best, subtly masking blemishes and accentuating your own colouring and features. When making-up, keep your hair away from your face and neck with a wide hairband. Face the daylight – electric light has a different, yellower quality. Start with clean hands and brushes, and have a supply of tissues. Tinted moisturiser is a light and soothing alternative to foundation. Whether or not you use foundation on the rest of your face, dab a little under your eyes and blend it in with a wedge of soft sponge to disguise the dark lines there. Use eye colour to highlight your natural bone structure, perhaps giving a little added weight and shape to eyebrows. Mascara needs to be

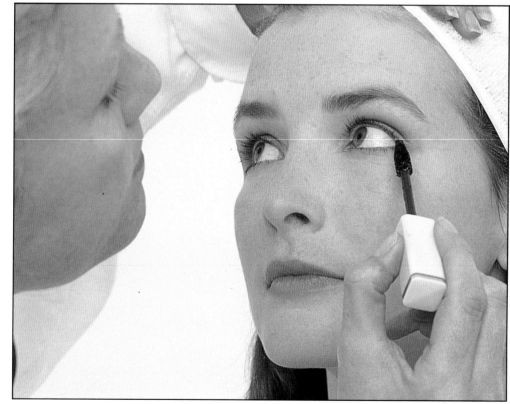

handled with special care so that your eyelashes are individually coated. Consider wearing a waterproof mascara if you think you might shed a tear of emotion on your wedding day. Be restrained with colour, but remember that a white or ivory wedding dress can make you look pale if you already have a cool complexion. All in all, be yourself – your fiancé is marrying you not a model from the pages of a magazine.

HAIR

Your hair will make an important contribution to the way you look and feel on your wedding day and like all aspects of your appearance it will repay the time and trouble you spend on it in previous months. Your overall diet and health will show in the quality of your hair and so will the care you take looking after it.

The best guide to beautiful hair is: keep it simple. The less you mess around with it the better. Perms, highlights, colouring can all make a contribution if used with a light touch and applied by experts but you are probably better off without. The most important thing is cut. A good cut is a good investment. A mediocre cut cannot be disguised by any amount of styling. Fussing about with it will probably make it look worse, not better. The ideal is a cut which gives your hair sharpness and shape; a cut which allows you simply to wash and condition your hair and let it dry naturally.

The cry 'I can't do anything with my hair!' usually really means 'I wish my hair were like someone else's: thicker/finer/fairer/darker/longer/shorter'. Some of these things you can do something about, some you can't. Getting married provides a good opportunity to take an honest look at many aspects of oneself and decide to like them. Your fiancé likes them – enough to marry them – so you can too. Look postively at your hair and go to the best hair-cutter in town – better than you think you can afford. He or she will be able to take a fresh look at your hair and give you a cut that makes the most of its best features.

When you have your hair cut for the first time after you have become engaged, discuss your wedding appearance with the hair-cutter. Take him or her a drawing of the design of your dress (the neckline is especially important) and if you are having your dress made, take her a swatch of the fabric. Tell her about your ideas for your style and weight of head-dress and veil and ask her advice.

If you want to change the style or cut of your hair, do it well in advance of your wedding so that you have time to get it just right and so that the look becomes part of you. After all, you want to look like yourself, not like an advertisement for hair products. On the other hand, this is the time for fulfilling your dreams. If you have always had a vision of yourself coming up the aisle with your hair up, decorated with flowers, there's nothing to stop you from doing it. If you want professional help with your hair on the day, book it in advance.

Consider your weekly hair routine. Do you wash your hair every day and do you always use the same shampoo? If so, you might like to make some changes. The less often you have to wash your hair the better – it shouldn't need washing every day. Some people go for a week or ten days before their hair loses its body. Using the same shampoo for months at a time can cause deposits to build up – keep two or three types of shampoo on the go at any one time and switch between them. Look for a high-rinsability shampoo. And when you wash your hair, give it a thorough rinse, right to the roots, in clean warm water. Lack of proper rinsing can be a cause of lank hair and itchy scalp.

Do you blow-dry your hair, or use heated rollers on it? Heat, whether natural or man-made, can be damaging to hair just as it is to skin, and should be avoided. If you are going on honeymoon to a hot country you should consider taking a special conditioner to protect it from the sun. Salt and chlorine should be washed out as soon after swimming as possible.

Take your hairbrush or comb and show it to your hair-cutter. She may be able to recommend a type which will suit your hair better. Thick hair, for example, is often best not brushed at all but combed with a wide-toothed comb. Hair can be brittle and needs to be treated gently. Rigid plastic brushes can do damage. She will also be able to advise you about when you should wash your hair for the wedding. Some types of hair are more controllable the day after they have been washed. If you have a mid-morning wedding there may not be time to wash it that day.

Caroline's hair is long and thick, in excellent condition and full of life. For her wedding she needs only follow her usual routine, conditioning and rinsing carefully. With her low-backed dress she could wear her hair in any one of a variety of styles. The simplest is swept back from her face and hanging straight down behind. The classic chignon is beautifully elegant and sophisticated but can be tricky if your hair tends to frizz. A third alternative is to plait it and knot it in a bun at the nape of the neck. Flowers can be entwined with your hair in any of these styles. Remember to consider your hair style when choosing a type of head-dress, and vice versa. Without plenty of experience and practice, and for relaxed self-confidence on the day, you will probably need professional help creating any of these three apparently simple styles.

5
STYLE

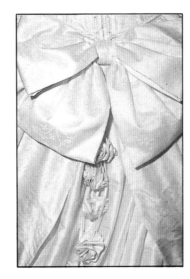

FINE FABRICS AND LACE

Let all your dreams come true. Exquisite sheer silks and satins, edged with a delicate froth of lace, make you feel and look like a princess. Dignified and dainty, these dresses follow classic lines which women through the ages have found flattering and comfortable. Think of yourself as the heroine of a romantic novel, about to be swept into marriage by a strong but tender man who has won your heart with valiant deeds. You are his dream come true – the soft fluttering of lace at your sleeve, an echo of your trembling heart. On your wedding day, fantasy and reality can overlap, wrapping you in finest fabrics. If you are traditional at heart and in love with the very best materials, these dresses are for you.

SUNSHINE DAYS

Cool cotton and crisp silks with
clever detailing for maximum
effect and comfort. Against the
bright blues of a Mediterranean
sea and sky, white looks more
brilliant than ever. In an English
summer, bright sunlight can be
just as dazzling – and so can
you. Forthright and fervent,
these styles and fabrics bring out
the best in a straightforward
character. They brook no
messing about, no dithering at
the church door, no holding
back from the simple joys of
life. Cut-out piqué and *broderie
anglaise* give extra interest to
cotton, a fabric favoured for its
honest simplicity. Lace is always
romantic and so are bows and
flowing skirts. Natural fibres
and natural complexions – ideal
if you are the outdoor type with
whom frills and fussiness do not
find favour. Be cool and feel free.

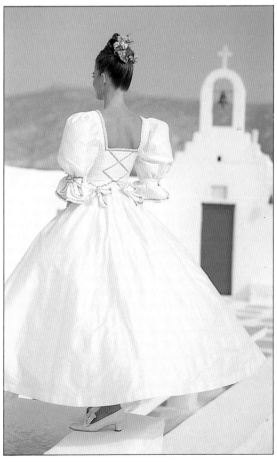

SWEET DREAMS

Pinks and peaches, stripes and frills. Silk or cotton seersucker is fresh and different, contrasting stripes and patterns add interest. You may feel the urge to make a departure from the usual white or cream, but not want to be married in plain blue or green, however subdued. Red or yellow is definitely too bold, and you don't want to wear a short dress to be married. These fabrics provide a solution. They are different to the usual, but not startlingly unusual. They lend themselves to classic styles and add something of their own – a touch of fun. Puff sleeves give importance to the top half of the dresses, while the lower half billows out into romantic, frothy layers of net petticoats and skirt. These dresses are pretty, soft and sweet.

GARDEN OF EDEN

Your dress can make you look faraway and ethereal, exquisitely unattainable and unworldly, existing in a dreamy world of your own. Or you can be an exotic bloom, firmly rooted in the ground but in touch with nature's forces and with the sap of passion running through your veins. Either way, these dresses will make you feel truly feminine. Above all they are soft. A dress like these will embrace you like a fairy's kiss, thrilling but light as a feather. They will be heaven to wear on your way to the altar and comfortable to dance in when you celebrate. Your husband will never have seen you looking so much like an angel or the most delicate flower in paradise, floating and fluttering in the breeze. For the bride who floats through life, these are dreamy gowns of silk and lace.

WINTER'S TALES

Like fire and ice, gleaming snowy satins and silks are edged with cosy fake fur, encrusted with rich embroidery, or lit up with brilliant red. In place of summer's floaty skirts and flirty frills, winter (and spring and autumn) offer serious elegance. The summer bride is a flower clothed in delicate petals; at other times a bride has to be prepared for cool weather and worse. She may in any case not be the flowery kind. There is as much fun to be had with strong fabrics as with floaty ones – they are just as beautiful but with different qualities. They lend themselves to clear definition – by themselves in a dress with clear-cut shape; or edged with fake fur or braid; or paired with a jacket or waistcoat of contrasting fabric and colour. Structure is everything, with heavy luxurious fabric, draped and pleated and tucked, but above all well-cut for form.

RICH AND RARE

These dresses combine a feeling of spiritual simplicity with the most sumptuous of fabrics. Their richly-textured damasks, lace, brocades and Jacquards in clotted cream, gilt and silver white evoke memories of medieval banquets and renaissance courts where nobility and courtiers expressed their loyalty to great kings and celebrated glorious victories; they speak of great heroines of literature, proud women of gentle birth whose lives were as rich as these fabrics. In such a dress, you will stand serene and reflective, amidst the bustle and noise of your marriage celebrations. These dresses are stately and magnificent, heirlooms of great value to be treasured by generations to come. Your inner self may be adjusting to your life's greatest change; but on the outside you exude calm sophistication and confidence.

BOLD AND BRILLIANT

These are for brides of strong character. The silhouette is classic and firmly defined, with shaped waists and sleeves which taper to elbow and wrist. The feeling is formal, upright, historic with drama dictating the detail. Acres of pure white and ivory are nothing new, but here they are offset by dashing tartan jackets and bodices, cuffs and bows, or by strong, contrasting embroidery and pattern. Take your colour lead from a piece of family jewellery you plan to wear at your wedding, a tiara perhaps, or a pendant, or from the stone in your engagement ring. If it's an emerald, be aware that green is supposed to be an unlucky colour for a wedding; but only the superstitious bride needs believe that story. With a real Scottish connection, your choice is all but made. Otherwise, follow your instinct for a dynamic wedding dress. Black and white or richly coloured, the plaids and patterns speak of daring adventures, highwaymen, history and passion.

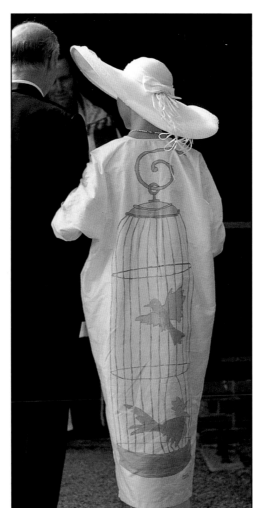

VIVE LA DIFFERENCE

Your wedding dress reflects the way you are. If short skirts are you, why not wear your kind of dress when you get married? If you are a double-breasted type, go for it. If red is your colour, wear it. If your spiritual home is in another continent or another century, let your wedding dress follow your heart on the day you give it away. Your wedding day is yours and it is up to you to set the mood by wearing whatever will make you happy.

CHOOSING A DRESS TO SUIT

When you see yourself in your imagination coming up the aisle, floating on a sea of shimmering organza, is it really you? Are you seeing yourself as you are, or imagining a perfect example of womanhood with your face added on? Models from the pages of fashion magazines do get married, but most of us have figures which are not quite as skinny and perfectly proportioned. Fortunately, the man you are marrying knows and loves you as you are. Your shape is part of what makes you who you are, and you want your wedding dress to minimise its less wonderful features and accentuate its best. The first step towards finding a dress to suit you is to establish exactly what these features are.

Take your clothes off and examine yourself as objectively as possible in front of a full-length mirror, somewhere warm so that you are comfortable and can take your time. Be realistic about your figure, looking for the positive points. Do you have a long neck and beautiful shoulders? Fine, taut arms? A small waist . . . long legs . . . elegant ankles? What are your worst points? Do you have chubby hips . . . a large bottom . . . thin arms? When you have made your mental list, commit it to memory and bear it in mind when you go shopping or discuss your dress with your dressmaker. Recall it too when looking at fashion photographs; the drop-waist, sleeveless beaded 1920s style dress looks fabulous on the model, but would it do justice to your fuller figure?

Looking at historical costume and twentieth-century fashion books in your local library can help you choose the dress to suit your personal style. Fashion designers often take their inspiration from history and certain classic shapes reappear again and again over the centuries. An Empire-line dress with high waist and soft draped skirt may be just the thing for you or the answer to your dreams might be a bodice and rustling bustle.

Trying on wedding dresses in a specialist shop or department is an enjoyable way of discovering the choice of styles and re-evaluating what exactly suits you. Shop assistants should be helpful and patient – after all you may spend a large sum of money in their shop – and are often extremely knowledgeable. Tell them what styles you have in mind and which parts of you you want to accentuate. They will bring you armfuls of dresses to try, some of which may give you new ideas for shape or fabric. Be open-minded – you thought you wanted a long dress but try on some short ones anyway.

Height is a factor which some people worry about. If you are short and your fiancé is tall the difference may be considerable. A train will give you added length, and a short, frothy veil could add height. But this doesn't alter your actual difference in height, and anyway your family and friends are used to it. Unless you are unduly worried it need not dramatically influence your choice of dress. If you are tall, perhaps taller than your fiancé, this too is a fact of life which can only be superficially disguised and of which you have no reason to be ashamed. Choose flattish shoes but don't stoop. If you tend to the broad, avoid gathers and pleating. Simplicity of either line or fabric (or both) is a good guide whatever your figure – you don't want frills distracting from your face.

An especially large or small bosom can be a source of concern. Be positive. If you are small bosomed you can wear a Gone-With-the-Wind style dress with a magnificent bow on the front, a deep puritan collar or a classical column of draped crêpe de Chine which a large girl cannot. If you are large bosomed, don't be apologetic. You have an asset which many girls will envy and you can wear a lower or more interesting neckline and more fitted bodice than someone with a lesser embonpoint. You should perhaps avoid sleeves which are full from shoulder to elbow, but you can equally well wear a dress with a straight or a full skirt. A long dress will probably look better on you than a short one, which would better suit a more flat-chested bride.

Slim, well-shaped legs and fine ankles can obviously be shown off under a short or mid-length dress, or you could save them for a stunning short-skirted going-away outfit. If you are proud of your arms a short-sleeved or sleeveless dress is ideal, and if you are marrying in winter the sleeves of your dress could be lace or chiffon to show off your arms. Winter brides can still wear the dress of their dreams – the excitement of the day will keep them warm. For added warmth you could invest in some silk or fine woollen underwear, or have your dress made in a natural-fibre, heavier weight fabric like silk duchesse satin.

The range of fabrics in which wedding dresses are made increases constantly. Designers take pleasure in working with new fabrics, and they also extend the range by supporting apparently delicate fabrics with backings and linings which give them the necessary body. The best way to discover the choice is to explore the specialist shops. Silk and satins are favourites all year round, with cotton, supported by petticoats and linings, joining them in summer. Silk can be fine and easily crushed like paper taffeta or heavy and soft like duchesse satin. Thai silk varies in weight from floaty and shiny to heavy and matt. In general, the heavier the fabric the less easily it creases. A recent royal bride who wore silk looked irredeemably crushed when she climbed down from the carriage, but in a few minutes the weight of the specially woven English silk had released the creases, leaving her dress looking fresh as new.

Cotton has the advantage of being cool, and has more variety than many people realise: cotton piqué, broderie anglaise, spotted cotton, seersucker and cotton jacquard are all possibilities. It is also generally less expensive than silk and satin. In a tropical climate – if you are planning a wedding abroad, in the Caribbean for instance – synthetics can be better than natural fibres because they do not crease in heat and humidity though they may breathe less well. Man-made fabrics are considerably cheaper than natural fibres and often look very similar, although they don't feel as good to wear.

An important consideration when choosing your dress is a detail not so much of your figure but of your whole person: the tone of your skin. If you are red-headed with a freckled complexion you can wear any shade of white and cream but rich ivories and golds will look especially wonderful. Pink would not be your best colour, but you can wear pale shades of blue and green (the latter if you are not superstitious). If you (or your fiancé) tend to have a more yellow complexion avoid bright white and go for a softer, creamier tone. If you have pale skin and dark hair and eyes, warm tones will bring colour to your cheeks. Blond hair and blue eyes are accented by bluish tones. Brown and black skin look dramatic with any colour in a very pale shade and softer with rich ivories and yellowy creams. Remember to look at yourself in daylight when trying on wedding dresses – electric light changes the tone both of your skin and of fabric.

The building where you are to be married has some bearing on your style of dress. A huge skirt or long train are appropriate in a cathedral or large church but not in a small chapel, where something more modest is in keeping, or at a register-office wedding when a shorter dress or suit is better. It is really a matter of common sense, and tact.

VEILS AND HATS

For centuries, no bride's appearance has been considered complete without her head being covered or decorated. Veils and hats have been in and out of fashion in turn, but during the last 150 years the emphasis has been on veils. The fashion is believed to have begun with the Romans. A Roman bride wore an enveloping yellow veil until safely in her new home on her wedding night, when her bridegroom removed it. In Anglo-Saxon times this was replaced with a 'care cloth', a square of cloth held over the head of the betrothed couple by four people with the purpose being the same as in Roman times: to conceal the bride's blushes from the people witnessing her betrothal or marriage.

In the eighteenth century, hats took over from veils, which returned in the early nineteenth century and were sometimes referred to as 'scarves'. Queen Victoria confirmed the trend with her veil of Honiton lace, and in 1854 a Norfolk vicar wrote in his diary about the excitement caused locally by a bride wearing 'a *veil*, supposed to be the first ever seen in Dereham'. Brides today are less likely to be blushing than smiling confidently, but a veil still adds an air of romance and mystery, softening the lines of your face and dress, and billowing or draping gracefully.

There is an enormous choice of weights, materials and colours of fabric, before you begin to decide on a length and style of veil. The six considerations when choosing your veil are: fabric, colour, detail, length, style and attachment. You should also consider the length of your hair. If it is thick and long a simpler and longer type of veil will be less fussy than a shorter fuller one.

Shorter hair looks good with almost any veil. The starting points for choosing are your personal preferences and the colour and style of dress.

FABRIC AND COLOUR

Veils are made of lace or a type of net or a combination of the two – net with a border of lace. Net is the most popular veiling. It is inexpensive and is made in a wider range of colours than any other veiling fabric, including white, cream and palest shades of pink, blue and green to match every imaginable hue of wedding dress. It is possible to find cotton net but most is nylon which doesn't crease – a definite advantage. Nylon net is slightly rough and stiff and

ideal for gathering onto a comb or band. Silk tulle is softer, lighter and more fluid – the fabric itself has smaller holes than net – and is considered the most flattering type of veiling. Its disadvantages are that it is expensive and it creases. It has to be well ironed and once your veil is in place you will have to try not to touch the area in front of your face, until the time comes to throw it back. There are two other fabrics – chiffon and georgette – which hang well and are sometimes, but more rarely, used as veiling. Chiffon is almost transparent and billows beautifully while georgette is heavier and less transparent. Georgette in particular is not ideal for wearing over the face.

ANTIQUE VEILS

Lace is perhaps the most romantic veiling of all. Bought new it is likely to be extremely expensive, but you may be able to buy an antique lace veil from an antique shop or market at an affordable price. Ideally, your family or your fiancé's family will have a lace or lace-edged veil from a previous generation, carefully preserved in a box in the attic during the years in which it was out of fashion or merely out of use. Even the most carefully stored family veil may need some careful attention before you can wear it. The Royal School of Needlework in London undertakes repair work on antique veils – take it to one of their workshops for advice and an estimate of the cost of restoration. If the colour of the veil is different to your wedding dress they can also undertake to tint it so it matches your dress as nearly as possible. If the veil is simply dirty you can wash it in tepid water and reputable cool-water liquid soap for wools and delicate fabrics, rinsing it gently and thoroughly. The alternative is to send it to a specialist dry cleaner.

An antique veil can emerge from storage stained and marked, and if you want to restore its whiteness you could try soaking your veil in one part hydrogen peroxide (20 vol) to 20 parts of water for no longer than 20 minutes before rinsing it carefully. To restore the stiffness either use a non-aerosol spray starch or soak it in gum arabic solution, leave it to dry for about 15 minutes then iron it with a cool iron. The recipe for gum arabic solution is: wash 4 ounces of gum arabic crystals in cold water. Add the crystals to one pint of hot water in a saucepan and dissolve them slowly over a low heat, stirring frequently. When they have melted, strain the liquid through fine muslin and bottle it. Before rinsing your veil, dilute this liquid in the ratio of one teaspoon to each two pints of water.

DETAIL

Many wedding-dress designers make net and tulle veils which match their dresses in colour, style and detail. Edgings are scalloped, sewn with tiny pearls or embroidered with flowers, bows or leaves, echoing details of the dress. You can also buy decorated veils like these separately from the dress, for example, a spotted net veil can look pretty with a simple dress. If you don't have an antique veil in the family you could look upon the cost of buying one as an investment in a new family heirloom.

LENGTH AND STYLE

Your veil can be any length from shoulder length to what is called 'cathedral length', extending out over a long train or for some distance behind your dress. Certain styles of veiling look better with types of dress – a short, full and frothy veil with a 1950s style three-quarter-length dress with nipped-in waist and full A-line skirt, for example. The shape of a veil does not always have to echo the shape of the dress. A slim, long, draped dress could equally well take a long, heavy silk veil or a short, gathered, frothy veil. But in general a veil looks most natural if its length is in proportion to the length of the dress.

Any discussion of the length of your veil

is complicated by the fact that a veil can be several lengths attached to each other. From the back of your head a long piece of net can billow out behind you, overlaid with a medium length piece which gives body to the first, with a short piece on top of these, perhaps attached to the front of your head-dress if it is a circlet. This part hangs down over your face and is thrown back or, if it has been lightly tacked, removed completely in the vestry during the signing of the register. This is an elaborate but effective arrangement. At the opposite end of the scale is a simple veil, possibly antique, which is a single square or round of fabric. It can either hang down at equal length all round your head, or the body of the fabric can be moved backwards so that a small part hangs in front and the rest behind. If the latter, it may be long enough to extend beyond the hem of your dress like a train.

FIXING YOUR VEIL

How you fix your veil partly depends upon your head-dress and your hair. You will know from experience with what ease or difficulty combs and slides stay securely in your type of hair. Imagine a small weight attached to them and you will be able to assess the problem. If your veil is being made for you it can be sewn to your head-dress. This is the most secure arrangement but has the disadvantage that you cannot remove the veil without the head-dress during the reception or party following your marriage. If your head-dress is to consist of fresh flowers delivered on the day, your veil can either be sewn to it

Brides over the centuries have
traditionally had their heads covered
by flowers, a veil, a hat or other
head-dress. Fashions come and go: in
the eighteenth century hats were
generally more popular while today it
is more usual to have a veil. Hats
therefore give you the opportunity to
be original and distinctive. A pretty
spring straw hat decorated with fresh
country flowers or a magnificent silk
hat laden with roses or swathed in
chiffon can be just as beautiful as a
veil and head-dress. Don't feel
confined to white if your dress is
another colour. If you prefer to wear
a veil, consider all the possibilities.
Veils can be long and flowing,
draping poetically around your face
and figure, or they can be short and
lacy. They can be drawn under your
chin or thrown back from your face.

quickly when it arrives or be fixed in your hair with combs.

A single comb in the middle will almost certainly not be enough – two or three are more reliable and will help prevent your veil becoming twisted. A delicate antique veil may be damaged by being sewn on to a head-dress, whether made from fresh or silk flowers, in which case combs are the answer. Sew the veil carefully to combs which are as nearly as possible the same colour as your hair, using lightweight thread which matches the tone of the veil. The combs may grip sufficiently well by themselves or you can use hairpins or kirby grips to create a fixture for them (fix two in your hair in a cross and slide the comb into the hair in front). Beware of hairpins and kirby grips coming loose and showing. However you fix your veil, be sure to leave enough hanging forward to cover your face and neck at the least.

Alternatively, you could wear a veil that hangs at the back only. There is no need for it to cover your face at all – it is entirely a matter of preference. The advantage of this arrangement is that once your veil is in place you can forget about it and need not worry about the business of deciding how the front part is to be organised and attached before the wedding, or about throwing it back and ensuring it is tidy afterwards during the wedding.

If you decide on a silk veil and it does somehow become creased just before the wedding, don't despair. Steaming will release the creases – the steam coming either from a boiling kettle or from a hot shower or bath run in a small room. Be careful not to scald yourself.

IN CHURCH

The point at which the bride traditionally lifts the veil from her face is after the marriage itself, during the signing of the register. Some brides remove their veil when they arrive at the chancel steps at the beginning of the service, but in this case there seems little point in wearing a veil over the face at all. The chief bridesmaid should be alert at all times to the possibility of a long veil becoming twisted or tangled and help the bride smooth it out at an appropriate moment. During the signing of the register you will need help throwing the veil back from your face or, if it is a separate piece which has been lightly tacked to your head-dress, removing the face veil completely (your mother could keep a pair of small scissors in her handbag to snip the thread). If you have a silk veil, make sure your bridesmaid understands how easily crushed it is, and handles it with due care.

HATS

Veils are currently the fashion, but there is no rule saying that you have to wear one. If you are a hat person you could wear a hat instead of a veil, or even a hat with a face veil attached. The shape and size of your hat should be appropriate to your dress. For a winter wedding you could wear an upright, Russian style hat made from snowy fake fur or velvet. With a long, full-skirted dress you could wear an Edwardian style hat with a wide boxy crown swathed in chiffon and silk flowers. Or you could have a hat made from the same fabric as your dress and decorate it with fresh flowers. A wide brim takes more flowers more securely than a small brim and by shading your face will give you the same air of mystery and romance as a veil. Be sure, however, that your face will be seen in the photographs. The photographer will probably be expecting you to wear a head-dress and veil – he may never before have photographed a bride wearing a hat. Warn him in advance that you will be wearing a hat so that he is prepared.

PRACTICE

Whatever you decide to wear, practising beforehand will give you added confidence on the day. It may also reveal any problem with fixing your hat or veil in place. This is the time when good posture is an asset. Keep your head up, think tall, and walk with measured steps of even length. Don't rush. Walking with your veil firmly in place, even when its just a practice, you will feel like a queen.

There are many alternatives to a head-dress made of fresh flowers. Silk and fabric flowers are the first to consider. They have several advantages over fresh flowers: they will not wilt or fade, the exact flowers you will wear can be chosen weeks in advance, and your head-dress can be made to fit you perfectly with no need for last minute adjustments.

You can also be sure that the colour will exactly match your dress. It is also possible to have a head-dress of flowers made from the same fabric as your dress, in the same or a contrasting colour and possibly matching similar flowers round the neck or on the back or train of your dress. Simple white or cream silk flowers make a beautiful circlet for you or your bridesmaids. Or you could even use silk and fresh flowers for a unique combination. If your silk flowers are formed into a separate head-dress rather than wound into your hair, your veil can be attached to it in advance, and you can rehearse wearing them together for maximum confidence on your wedding day.

Dried flowers are an interesting alternative to fresh or silk ones. They are more delicate and brittle, but have many of the advantages of silk flowers. They can be arranged in advance, and are often available in richer and more mellow colours than silk and fabric flowers. Alternatively, dispense with flowers altogether. A family tiara borrowed for the occasion or an antique tiara made of wax beads will give you an air of majesty. If it is valuable be sure that you have suitable insurance cover so that it doesn't cause you or its owner any worries. If it has coloured stones, it could provide you with your wedding's colour theme.

Shoes must fit well and be truly comfortable; if you do not usually wear high heels, don't start now, even if you are much shorter than your groom. It is more important for your feet to feel comfortable as you will spend much of the day standing up and walking among your guests. Apart from questions of comfort, your wedding shoes can fulfil all your fantasies. They are your secret. Your shoes can be embroidered, appliquéed, painted, made from elaborate brocade, or be utterly simple but of an exquisite shape. You could buy them or have them specially made from the same fabric as your wedding dress; or specially decorated with your initial on one toe and your fiance's on the other, or entwined on both.

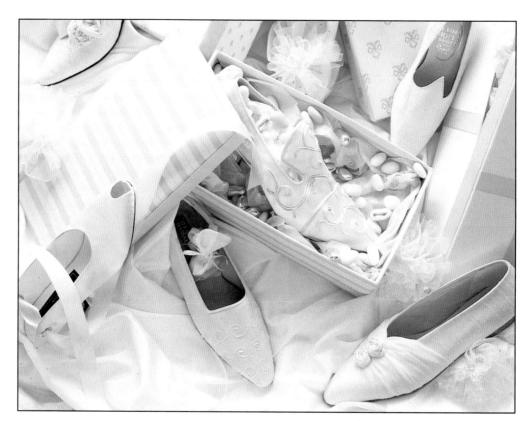

SHOES

Shoes are a bride's greatest luxury. Compared with your dress, your shoes are not a huge expense, even if you treat yourself to something really special. They must be fairly practical, but mainly they can fulfil your wildest dreams of romance and elegance.

The practical aspects concern size, height and the time of year. If you are getting married in the country in the middle of winter you might consider taking a slightly sturdier pair of shoes to change into which would get you from car to church and back again without your feet getting dirty or cold. Once in the church you can wear the daintiest slippers in the world. In most circumstances, however, you will be wearing your shoes from the moment you get dressed until you change go to away on your honeymoon, and they need to be just robust enough to cope with a light shower or a little summer dust.

You will be on your feet for a large, and certainly the most important, part of the day, so your shoes must fit. They must be comfortable, and their height should be similar to the height of heel you usually wear. Beware of high heels if you are not used to them. They may look sophisticated and glamorous but they can quickly become uncomfortable and could even damage your feet. Your honeymoon will be no fun if you are hobbling for days after the wedding.

Your shoes will be seen, but if you are wearing a long dress they will only be seen in glimpses. They can therefore be quite elaborate without making your overall appearance seem fussy. The most luxurious shoes are embroidered with coloured silks or tiny pearl beads, dancing and glittering in intricate patterns or cooly spelling your initial on the toe of each shoe. A generous silk rosette or bow on the toe, or a spray of feathers on the tongue, adds a touch of drama. The colours can be delicate, white or ivory or palest pink, in keeping with your dress, or they can include a splash of colour. Green leaves curling round your foot or a posy of warm, rosy pink silk flowers on one side will add dash to your outfit. The congregation may be able to

If you plan to have shoes specially embroidered or otherwise decorated, or if you want them dyed or made up in your own fabric, you should leave plenty of time, allowing an additional few weeks in case something goes wrong – you want your shoes to be perfect. And, remember, choose the shoes you want as, even if they're hidden by a long dress, you'll know they're there.

catch a glimpse of them when you kneel in church but otherwise they are your secret until the dancing starts. An antique or new buckle in silver or diamanté can transform a simple shoe. Or stitch a flamboyant pearl ear-ring to the front.

The alternative is the saintly, virginal wedding shoe, exquisite in shape, perhaps with a curved Louis heel, but covered in undecorated white satin. Plain shoes like these are generally inexpensive and can be dyed to match the exact tone of your wedding dress fabric, or left in their original gleaming white. The best-known producers of fabric-covered shoes are suppliers of dancing shoes who are expert in dying shoes to an astonishingly accurate match and who will also sometimes make their design of shoes in your own fabric. This could be the same fabric as your dress, or it could be a luxurious floral brocade or damask in colours which tie in with your flowers. Leave extra time for dying and more still for shoes in special fabric. These shops are the obvious place to buy bridesmaids' shoes too, to be dyed to match their dresses. Other specialist shops have extra wide or long shoes suitable for brides with large feet.

You need not wear shoes at all, if you prefer boots. Elegant lace-up ankle boots made from white kid or a fabric to match your dress would go well with a Victorian or Edwardian style of dress. Most daring of all, wear fabric-covered shoes that you have decorated yourself or a friend has decorated for you with fabric paints or pens. These can be used in their original strong colours or diluted with water for cool pastel shades.

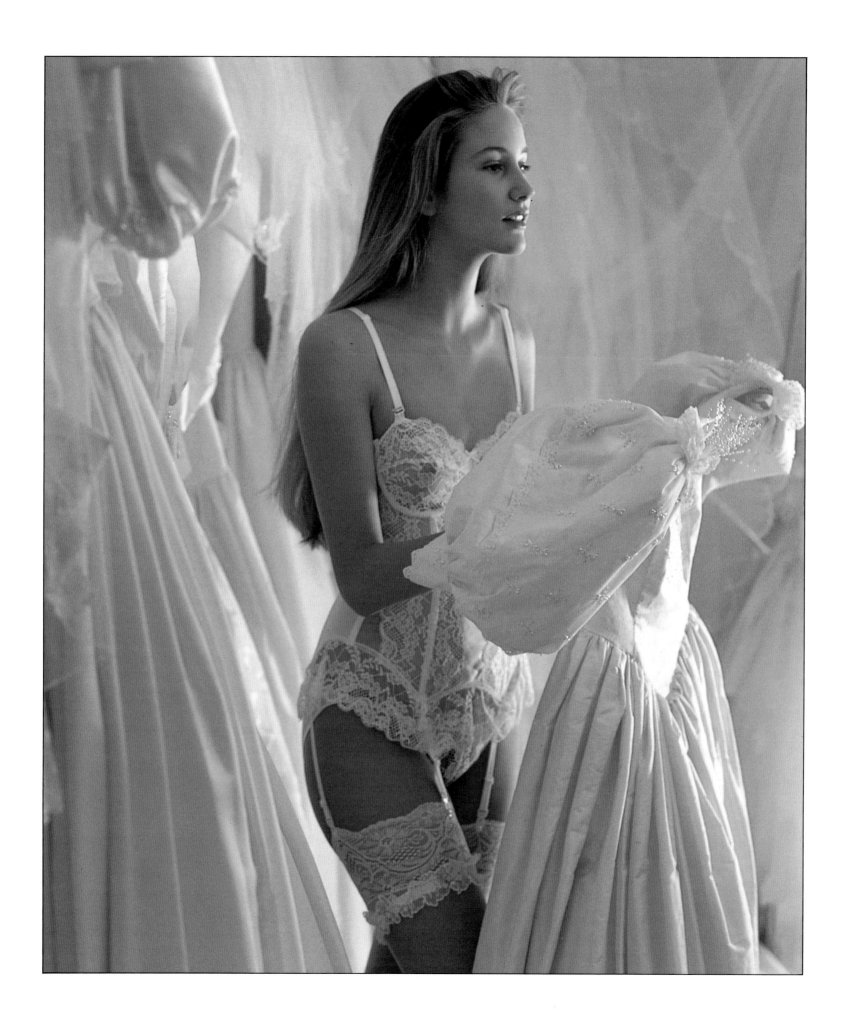

UNDERWEAR

Your usual underwear, clean and comfortable, is perfectly suitable for your wedding day and you should certainly not feel you have to buy something new for the occasion. On the other hand, if you have always hankered after silk camiknickers and never felt the expense was justified, indulge yourself now. Plain white or cream underwear is more appropriate than brightly coloured knickers or a black lacy bra for wearing under your wedding dress, though even these will do, if there is no chance of them showing. Your dress may require a special undergarment such as a basque or strapless or backless bra. But other than this, your underwear is a matter of taste – your taste. No one can tell you that it is or is not correct to wear one type of underwear or another.

The one part of you which is under your dress but which will almost certainly show is your legs and feet. For a subtle effect your tights or stockings want to be exactly the same shade as your dress or lighter, not darker. Some rich creamy shades of ivory and tones of palest pink are difficult to match so go shopping for tights as soon as your dress or dress fabric has been chosen, taking a swatch with you. Remember when looking at packets that the colour is paler and sometimes looks quite different once on your leg, so try the tights on as soon as you get home. Don't leave it until the day of your wedding.

Under a long dress with a full skirt you can be a little more daring in your choice of tights or stockings. Pale shades of blue, pink and green, tying in with the colour theme of your wedding, can look pretty under a wedding dress. Warm lacy tights in white or cream are a luxurious alternative if you are getting married in winter.

If you don't normally wear stockings but want to wear them at your wedding, practise in advance as they do feel different to tights. Instead of tights or stockings, you could wear stocking socks, under a long dress. They are easy to manage during the day and are cool and comfortable. If your wedding dress is ankle length or above so that your ankles and some of your leg shows, ask your mother or best friend to keep a spare pair of tights in her bag in case of a ladder. You could do this whatever your length of dress.

Most wedding dresses are sold with all the necessary petticoats and underskirts, but some are not, and you might in any case like to give extra fullness to your

chosen dress with some added layers of net. Be careful not to add too much bunchy fullness at the front – the back is a better place for this. Alternatively, build the net up in layers on yolks, so that the fullness increases as the petticoat descends. Net can be cut and gathered without edging, but it may need a silky lining so that the cut edges do not tear tights or stockings or tickle your bare legs.

The alternative is to bind the bottom edge of each layer of underskirt with satin ribbon – a laborious job, and the ribbon will detract from the lighter-than-air look of the layers of net. Net can be hemmed by being machined with the cut edge outermost, but this too can detract from its appearance.

If your net underskirt is separate from your dress, consider hanging it upside down before the wedding. This will encourage it to puff out rather than lie flat on the day.

As important as your wedding day, where underwear is concerned, is your honeymoon and the months thereafter. Just as you hope your new husband will not subject you to his old favourites – so you should take a fresh look at your own underwear. What would you **like** him to see you in? On a practical level, does your knicker drawer simply need a new lease of life? Take this opportunity to throw away all your tired and worn underwear. Now you have an excuse to invest in some sparkling new underwear that will thrill him as much as you. Buy him some new boxer shorts too, to nudge him in the direction of disposing of his ragged old ones, if he hasn't already thought of doing so himself.

DRESSING BRIDESMAIDS AND PAGEBOYS

It is easy to be overcome by the excitement of choosing your wedding dress and temporarily forget that your attendants' appearance is just as important in creating a total look for your wedding. Not only do you want them to look wonderful by themselves, but their clothes need to complement your own dress and their colours blend with the overall theme of the wedding. Bridesmaids and pages also tend to be dressed with more attention to the time of year than does the bride herself. This is a positive point – winter bridesmaids in tartan or scarlet and green are just as decorative as floral spring and summer ones. In fact the colours you choose for your attendants can set the theme for the whole wedding, if the inspiration has not already come from elsewhere.

Make sure their tones, especially white or cream, harmonise with your own dress. Colours should be of similar warmth – not ice blue if your dress is rich ivory, for instance. The fabric of their clothes needs to be considered too. If your dress is heavy satin avoid raw silk, for example, as it falls differently as well as having a different colour quality and finish.

What they wear also depends to some extent on your attendants' ages. Your contemporaries will look and feel happier in a type and style of garment which you yourself could wear, while small girls look enchanting in variations of the classic puff-sleeved, full skirted dress with sash. Pageboys present a slight problem in that they are notorious for becoming dishevelled. It isn't fair to expect small boys to keep completely still throughout the preparations and journey to the church so there is a danger that a shirt will come untucked here, a cuff button be pulled off there, and so on. Mostly this can be rectified by their mothers or your best friend waiting for them at the church door, but some of the worry is removed if you can devise an all-in-one outfit, eliminate elements of their outfit which ask for trouble, or attach the separate parts in advance with safety pins or Velcro.

In other ways, pageboys offer more scope than bridesmaids. They can be dressed in tribute to your or your fiancé's profession or interests, in sailor suits, miniature uniforms, period costume or kilts. Little girls offer the imagination scope for romance in miniature, sweet and adorable. In spring and summer they can be dressed in light, floaty fabrics or crisp cotton, plain or patterned with spots, stripes or delicate floral designs. In autumn and winter they can be more dramatic, in black and rust or scarlet and green. Florals can be bolder, both in size and colour. Or they can wear classic white dresses made with long sleeves and from heavier fabric, and with sashes and shoes in winter colours.

Your bridesmaids do not all have to be dressed identically. You could use the same design and fabric, but in four different colourways. Or each could be dressed in a different pastel shade. Or they could be dressed in matching pairs in the same fabric but different outfits, according to their ages. If your wedding has a theatrical theme because of your or your fiancé's interests or profession, you could dress each attendant as a recognisable character. Small bridesmaids and pages can be dressed as animals or cherubs, but if you are going to do something this unusual you must explain the reasoning behind it to your minister first and gain his approval so that he doesn't get an awkward surprise on the day.

By the same token, bridesmaids do not have to wear floral head-dresses and carry posies. Their circlets or Alice bands can be formed from herbs and foliage or heads of wheat at a summer wedding, holly (a prickle-free variety), ivy and berries at a winter wedding. They could wear hats decorated with ribbons or flowers or made from crushed velvet or fake fur or, if you are lucky enough to have bridesmaids with glorious hair, their heads could be uncovered. A mass of deep brown, golden or russet Pre-Raphaelite curls needs no adornment. They can carry miniature Christmas trees or hoops of fir and ivy decorated with bright ribbons in winter, sheafs of country flowers or baskets of fruit in summer. Pageboys don't usually carry anything, but if you wish they could hold prayer books or small caskets containing rose petals or confetti. Don't give them anything too fragile or precious – it's not fair to expect them to take as much care as an adult might.

Adult bridesmaids should be dressed as simply as possible. Don't ask them to wear anything you wouldn't wear yourself. It would be courteous to ask them in advance if there is a colour which they really dislike and doesn't suit them – you want them to be as happy and relaxed as you are on your wedding day.

A simple, fresh look is ideal for bridesmaids of any age. Sweep hair off their faces, keep jewellery and make-up to a minimum, and let their healthy glow shine through. Whatever they wear, keep in mind the overall colour theme of your wedding, and relate the style of their dresses to yours.

When you plan your attendants' clothes, there are various matters to consider. The most obvious is the way they look: you want them to continue the theme begun by your own dress, both in outline and in detail. If you are wearing an off-white colour you want to be sure the background to a floral print tones in with this, and you want the outline and style of your bridesmaids' dresses to be similar to yours. Remember too that your bridesmaids and pageboys must look ravishing from every angle as your friends and family will see more of their backs than their fronts during the service. There are also practical considerations, such as the time of year the wedding is going to take place and the age of the attendants. It is usual for the bride's father to meet the cost of the outfits. If you can't manage this and want your attendants to pay for their own clothes, you must consult them about what they are to wear and give them a real choice.

Dress them as elves and pixies or as miniature Pre-Raphaelite beauties. Your attendants can wear floaty lawn smocks or classic frocks with puffed sleeves. You should be sure, however, that your small attendants understand in advance what they will be wearing and are happy and comfortable in their clothes. You don't want any tantrums on the day.

Page boys' clothes can express a theme of the wedding or reflect your or your husband's work or interests – they can be dressed in an artist's smock and carrying a colourful palette, for instance, or, as here, wearing a sailor suit.

Another alternative is the miniature morning suit. Small bridesmaids look enchanting in almost anything. Try to arrange for them all to be at the rehearsal so that they are not overwhelmed by the size of the building and the splendour of the occasion on the day. When you ask their parents if their children can be your attendants make it clear what travelling will be required for shopping for and fitting their clothes.

Be daring in winter and summer. Strong colours and warm fabrics look stunning and will protect your bridesmaids from draughts and chills in winter; so will fake fur hats and muffs. Make the most of the weight and texture of wonderful fabrics like velvet and heavy silk. Combine them with a palette of vibrant colours such as ruby red, bottle green and gold, or with dashing tartan patterns. In summer have fun with floaty fabrics for girls and lacy ruffles for boys. Dress your pages in smart silk waistcoats or billowing regency coats. The classic dress for pageboys is britches and a plain or frilly white shirt, but beware of the gap that can develop between the two as energetic little boys wriggle in the car on their way to church. Someone needs to be ready to smarten them up if things have come adrift.

Grown-up bridesmaids can be dressed in similar clothes to their younger colleagues, or in a more sophisticated style that reflects their age and is closer to your own dress. Pattern and colour will enrich your entourage, especially in winter. Even black can be used to dramatic effect for details on your and your attendants' outfits; a black velvet riding jacket and hat worn over black-and-white plaid, for example. Tartan in deep, rich colours is equally impressive. If frills aren't your style, go for something bold and dynamic. Be sure, though, that your bridesmaids' and pages' appearance doesn't overpower that of the most important person at the wedding – you.

Fashions in shape and style of brides' bouquets change as much as their dresses do. Don't allow yourself to be dictated to by current fashion – think what you would really like. The huge cascading bouquet is only one option, albeit a popular and beautiful one. A rounder bunch is another possibility, incorporating groups of different, brightly-coloured blooms or sprinkled all over with delicate colours. If you decide on a scented bouquet, remember that this may limit your choice of flowers. Another possibility is a sheaf which you carry over one arm. White lilies make a magnificent sheaf, as do heads of wheat and decorative grasses. Flowers with shorter stalks are not so suitable. A bouquet can take unusual forms – your initial, for example, if it is suitably flowing – 'S' perhaps, or 'J'. Or you could carry your flowers in a basket, dispensing with the bouquet entirely. If you are lucky, you might find an antique silver posy-holder, such as the Victorians used, to grip the stalks and give a comfortable and elegant hand-hold.

THE BRIDE'S BOUQUET

Fresh flowers and foliage have been associated with weddings for as long as there have been weddings, and the custom of the bride carrying some sort of fresh greenery and flowers is almost as old. Herbs such as rosemary and garlic were carried to ward off evil spirits. Tudor brides carried rosemary which had been gilded and dipped in scented water, and at less wealthy weddings it was simply strewn beneath the feet of bride and groom. The Victorians were fascinated by the meaning of flowers' names. Today your choice of flowers and foliage for your wedding is almost unlimited. Flowers are flown around the world every day so that it is possible to get the most perfect tropical blooms as well as typically English flowers in the middle of winter.

Ideas about flowers have also changed within recent decades. A bride's choice is no longer limited to sophisticated and elaborate bouquets and the flowers no longer have to be virginal white. If you do choose white, be careful to match the colour with the fabric of your dress. Man-made fabrics can be a brilliant white which only a few flowers like carnations, hyacinth and some roses can match. You may prefer your flowers to be yellow, blue, pink, or even a brilliant mixture of bright pink, orange and red flowers like a ball of fire. Your bouquet can be the starting point for your wedding's colour theme or it can simply be made from the flowers you love most. Exotic hot-house blooms or a sheaf of country flowers . . . your choice is a reflection of your personal taste and feelings about your marriage.

Do not choose the flowers for your bouquet in isolation. It is easy to be dazzled by the colours available and by the exquisite perfection of the flowers, but it is important to think of your bouquet as one element in the overall look of your wedding. If your dress is rich in detail, you want a simple, bold bouquet rather than a fussy one, but if your dress is elegantly simple you can either carry a few perfect blooms which will emphasise that simplicity, or a gloriously elaborate bouquet which will add interest to your appearance. You must also consider your head-dress, your attendants' flowers and the flowers in the church and at the reception, and plan the whole effect all day through. The buildings where the ceremony and party afterwards are to be held are important too, both in terms of colour and style of arrangements. If in doubt it is better to err on the side of boldness and simplicity – decorous and very detailed arrangements can so easily be lost in a large church and amongst a crowd of friends and family in their colourful party clothes.

The three main forms in which you can have the flowers you carry are sheaf, bunch and bouquet. A sheaf consists of flowers (and foliage, grasses, etc.) with long stalks held together so that the flowers are all at one end. You hold the stalks in your hand with the flowers over the crook of your arm. A few lilies held together with ribbon can make a ravishing sheaf, and so can ripe heads of wheat, lavender and poppies. The stalks of flowers in a sheaf have to be long enough for you to be able to hold them with your arm relaxed, and should be neatly trimmed.

A bunch is round in shape, fairly flat on top and deep from back to front. The impact is equally well achieved with just two or three types of flower massed together, or with a collection of contrasting flowers bunched together in places within the bunch. The Victorians held bunches which they called 'tussie-mussies', backed with cut and embossed paper. They included sweetly scented flowers which made journeys in stuffy coaches and railway carriages more pleasant. A sophisticated bunch might consist of a solid mass of palest pink roses and tulips edged with red, while a more countrified bunch could include herbs and pretty flowers like blossoms, stocks, hydrangeas and guelder roses. Bright strong colours are shown off well by the plain shape of the bunch.

A bouquet (though strictly 'bouquet' means any selection of cut flowers designed to be held) is a variety of blooms cut and wired into a cascade. It can be any reasonable shape – heart-shaped or S-shaped, for instance, but the most popular is the inverted tear-drop shape. A formal bouquet like this can be pure white or cream with a touch of green and silver or gold, or it can combine different colours within the same tonal range to equally good effect – delicate pastels or soft shades of stronger colours, for example.

As with all the flowers at your wedding, you can either arrange them yourself or commission someone else – a friend or professional – or a mixture of the two. Arranging flowers takes time, possibly much longer than you might think, and it is unlikely that you yourself will be able to do them alone. You might manage with the help of a friend or relation whose taste and skill you trust, but only if you are experienced in working with flowers. Static arrangements should be finished the day before the wedding, to allow them time to settle securely before being checked on the day. This may mean starting the arrangements on the Thursday before a Saturday wedding, or earlier depending on how elaborate they are and how many arrangements are involved.

Doing some of the flowers yourself can save money and leave you more to spend on other things. Most wholesale flower markets, where prices are lower than florist shops, allow the public to buy there – especially if you are buying in bulk. Visit the market in advance to see the range of their regular stock, discuss your requirements and place an advance order, but go early as most

flower markets close well before lunchtime. Have a mass of water-filled buckets ready to receive the flowers when you get them home, and allow them a rest and a drink before you begin arranging them. If some of the flowers are being done by professionals, explain to them well in advance that you or a friend or relation are also doing some arranging, so that there is no misunderstanding later about exclusive access to the church and reception. Keep all wedding locations where there are flowers cool and shaded. Once your arrangements are complete, check them and spray them and the oasis with water at intervals to refresh them. Don't try cramming flowers into your refrigerator – they will only be crushed and wilt when brought out into the warmth.

FOLIAGE

Nothing sets off the velvet bloom and glowing colours of fresh flowers so well as abundant greenery, whether glossy and dark or feathery and silver-grey. Flowers' own foliage is the ideal, but often this has taken the brunt of travels and is bruised or broken. Some plants put everything into their flowers and have only insignificant foliage. You will probably have to buy, or even better find, foliage separately. Herbs, shrubs and trees are wonderful providers of foliage of every colour and texture, especially in our temperate climate. If you live in the country, you may find wild foliage to pick, but be sensitive about the quantity and position of greenery you take. Look for:

Laurel	Acers	Rue
Rhododendron	Ferns	Mint
Holly	Bamboo	Fennel
Ivy	Eucalyptus	Artemisia
Mistletoe	Pittosporum	*Euonymus fortunei*
Fruit trees	Rosemary	Hostas

SCENTED FLOWERS

The most famous scented flower associated with weddings is orange blossom which was at the height of popularity following Queen Victoria's wedding in the middle of the nineteenth century. Lily of the valley is perhaps the most popular scented flower today,

but is only one of many available. There is nothing so romantic as a cool and gloomy church filled with the scent of lilies or roses. In your discussions with your florist or at the flower market, make it clear if you want scented flowers. Blooms which have been developed for colour, size and long life do not necessarily have a scent, and the scent may also depend on their country of origin. Some roses from South America smell wonderful while the same type of rose grown in Holland does not have any scent at all.

If you or your fiancé has an elderly relative or a friend who cannot see or hear particularly well, you could make a posy or buttonhole of scented flowers for them to hold or wear, to help involve them in the joy of your wedding and diminish the sense of isolation experienced by people with poor sight and hearing.

Roses

Jane Packer, royal florist, suggests the following scented roses.

PINK	ORANGE	RED
'Carol'	'Belinda'	'Baccara'
'Rouletii'	'Mercedes'	LILAC
'YELLOW	'Flower Arrange'	'Blue Moon'
'Cocktail'	'Orange Sensation'	PEACH
WHITE	'Floribunda'	'Oceana'
'Athena'		

Other scented flowers

Her list of other flowers which are or may be scented includes:

Altenifolia	Honeysuckle	Pink Doris
Anthurium	Hyacinth	Rudbeckia
Chinese Witch	*Iris stylosa* 'Algerian'	Stephanotis
Hazel	Japonica	Stock
Chrysanthemum	Jasmine	Sweet Pea
carinatum	Lily	Tobacco Plant
'Northern Star'	Mignonette	(evening scent)
Freesia	'Goliath'	Viburnum
Gardenia	Narcissus	Wallflower
Gladiolus		

Continue the overall look of your wedding
when choosing a style of head-dress – it should
complement both your face and your dress.
Use it to keep your hair off your face so
everyone can see you, or entwine your hair
around it so that the two become one. If you
choose to have a head-dress in the form of a
wire circlet supporting fresh flowers,
remember to line it with dark velvet ribbon for
added comfort as your wedding day
progresses. The ribbon can simply be stuck to
it, silky side against the wire and soft side
outwards, with good quality glue. Allocate this
job to a member of your family who is good
with their hands – don't do it yourself and risk
spoiling your hands and nails on your wedding
day. A well-made circlet can be a considerable
weight of flowers and even fruit and still be
comfortable all day long. When deciding on a
style of head-dress made from fresh flowers,
discuss it in great detail with your florist. Be
careful with gypsophila – used cleverly it looks
romantically light and delicate, but if used too
sparingly it can look spotty.

FRESH FLOWER HEAD-DRESSES

Your head-dress should be planned in conjunction with your bouquet and all the other flowers for your wedding, in terms of both colour and design. Discuss your ideas for a floral head-dress with your hairdresser and florist before you decide, and bear in mind the type of veil you will be wearing. Your flowers can consist of a single bloom on one side of your head, or a magnificent crown of colour, or anything in between. An Alice band can add to your height; a spray fixing your veil above each ear has a 1920s appearance. Include some foliage for a pastoral look or some gypsophila for lightness. Foliage can make a magnificent head-dress by itself or with a scattering of flowers or berries – variegated holly with its own red berries and some Christmas roses for a winter bride, for example.

Remember that you will be wearing the head-dress for many hours so the measurement around your head needs to be accurate for a comfortable fit. Most types of head-dress can be adjusted slightly on the day, including full circlets. The wire mount can be formed into a hook and eye at the back rather than in an unending circle. If you are wearing a hat you can either have a full circle of flowers made to fit the crown, or take the hat (suitably wrapped for protection) to the florist in advance for the flowers to be attached.

FLOWERS FOR THE BRIDESMAIDS

The colours and types of flower which your attendants carry should complement your own and the floral scheme for the whole wedding. If your head-dress and bouquet are white or cream or a pale colour, consider giving them stronger colours or verdant foliage to carry, rosemary for remembrance, for example, and myrtle for love. If your own colours are rich and bright, theirs could be paler shades of the same. Their flowers must also be appropriate to their own clothes. If they are wearing silk, formal flowers like lilies, camellias and gardenias are suitable, but cotton and light fabrics like voiles and nets call for casual flowers such as sweet peas, pinks, violets and gypsophila.

Small children carrying large arrangements of sophisticated flowers can look overburdened. Give them flowers that are in proportion to their size and they will look, and be, more comfortable. They will also look more natural with country flowers and herbs rather than exotic hot-house blooms – keep those for yourself and the more senior bridesmaids. Older bridesmaids should carry larger posies – if they are too small they will look silly. An experienced florist will suggest sizes and types of arrangement. These could be traditional posies or, for smaller attendants, hoops or baskets of flowers and foliage, and even fruit. At a country wedding in summer, you could arrange clusters of hedgerow fruits amongst colourful flowers with their own leaves in small trugs for your bridesmaids to carry.

If you are looking for ways of cutting costs, you might consider having a professional make your head-dress and bouquet and perhaps your bridesmaids' head-dresses, which involve careful wiring and positioning of flowers, but arrange the flowers your attendants will carry yourself. Make simple bunches of perfect flowers, held together with florist's wire wound around each stalk and then decorated with a coloured ribbon, or construct baskets of flowers. Line the basket with plastic first for waterproofing, then fit an oasis so that it is taller than the base of the basket. This way the flowers and foliage stand up proud and can drape down over the sides.

Don't forget the groom and other men closely involved with the wedding. You should arrange buttonholes – a rose or a spray including heather, for example – for your fiancé, his father and yours, the best man and possibly the ushers and the person making the first toast at the reception, in a colour which ties in with your overall scheme. The groom pays for these together with other church flowers. Any guest who wants to wear a buttonhole arranges and pays for it themself.

LEFT Small bridesmaids need flowers they can happily manage to hold and which crown their heads without weighing them down.

LEFT A pompom of flowers can be held by a coloured ribbon, with no danger of the arrangement being held upside down.

Think bold and positive when planning your bridesmaids' flowers. They can be a riot of brilliant colour, or visions of delicate tones floating on airy gypsophila. Remember that they contribute to the overall look of your wedding, so continue your theme with particular types and colours of flower, fruit and foliage.

Bridesmaids' flowers must be comfortable to wear and easy to carry, especially for your small attendants. Brief them just before you all leave for the church, when they have their flowers in their hands, about how to hold them. If they have posies or small bouquets, they should relax their arms almost to their full length, and tip the flatter side of the flower arrangement forward so that it can be seen as they walk up the aisle.

Flowers outside the church welcome your relations and friends to the joyful occasion of your marriage. They are also there to greet you, when you arrive at church. A gate or porch is an obvious focus of attention, as people crowd round to enter, or wait for their service sheets.

FLOWERS OUTSIDE THE CHURCH

In late spring, summer and early autumn, when the weather is at its best and least unreliable, you can decorate not only the inside of the church but also the outside entrance. Your guests will be welcomed by an archway or swag of foliage and flowers, flower 'trees' each side of the door, or hanging arrangements trailing elegant streamers of ivy or smilax. The porch or area just inside the door can be transformed into a bower with plants in pots and arrangements of flowers and foliage.

To make a flower 'tree', fix a post into a large flowerpot, using enough plaster-of-Paris or stones to create a secure and solid weight which will prevent the tree from falling over. Alternatively, use a stone urn and pack the post securely with enough stones and soil to fix it in place and create sufficient weight. Wrap oasis around the top of the post with a length of chicken wire and fix securely to the post. This ball is then filled out with abundant foliage and flowers. Cover the plaster-of-Paris in the pot with moss or earth and decorate the post with ribbons. The pot can be covered with paper or fabric, or left bare if it is stone or a real terracotta pot and you like the colour.

FLOWERS INSIDE
THE CHURCH

A wedding is a joyful celebration of love and it is natural to want to make the place where your marriage is solemnised as beautiful as possible. Many churches and places of worship are magnificent buildings in themselves, but even here well-chosen flowers will increase the sense of occasion and excitement. The flowers do not have to be costly and elaborate – in a country church or small chapel a few vases of scented flowers can create the perfect atmosphere.

Before planning flowers for a church it is sensible and courteous to consult the minister. He knows about equipment available for flower arrangements (pedestals, vases and so on) and if he is observant he may be able to give you tips about quirks of the building like the way the light falls in the month or at the time of day when you are getting married. If there is a person who usually arranges or is in charge of flowers they too may be able to give you some ideas. They have probably seen the flowers for many weddings in that church and will remember the most successful.

In popular churches there may often be several weddings taking place on the same day in the summer months, in which case the church will have a policy about flowers. The vicar's wife or another person may arrange them, choosing white and cream for wedding days, and the cost is split between the various people being married.

Go to the church itself at a time when it is empty and wander around, looking at the window sills, the width of the aisle, the area inside the sanctuary and generally make yourself familiar with the building. Look for architectural features of the building to highlight with flowers – a beautiful arch, pulpit or column. If there is a screen dividing the choir area from the congregation and it has a wide top it may be possible to have flowers here, hanging down over the edge in a waterfall of colour. When you are in the congregation at a service in the church were you are to be married, make a mental note of good spots for large arrangements, and notice places where they would be obscured by your seated guests. As with all the elements

of your wedding, other people's weddings are the perfect hunting ground for ideas.

The amount of natural light in the building where you are getting married will influence the main colour of the flowers – in a dark building it is important to have pale colours, ideally white and cream, which will light up the church and be clearly seen. Deep rich colours will blend with the background and be lost. In a very light and airy building, pale colours can look stunning and so can strong bright ones. Pure white or cream might look washed out. Most churches and places of worship have a reasonable amount of natural light so that the colour of your flowers is entirely a matter of taste. Ask the minister about altar cloths, however. You may find you can take a lead for the colour scheme of your wedding from a particularly beautiful one available for weddings, or from some other decorative element in the church.

The obvious places for significant flower displays are on or at each side of the altar, each side of the chancel steps (taking into account the pulpit and lectern), the window sill directly opposite the entrance door, and the font. You can either concentrate on these areas, decorating them with large explosions of colour, or you can decorate other structural elements in the church as well for a more overall effect. Pillars, window sills and pew ends are favourites, though you need to take special account of the width of the aisle and your guests' view of you and your fiancé during the service if you hang flower arrangements here.

If the flowers are all quite low, however, there is the danger that none will be visible to the congregation when they are standing. It is better to have a few really tall and magnificent arrangements as well as, or instead of, many small ones which may get lost.

Check that there isn't a christening that weekend before planning to fill the font with flowers. Flowers on sills need plenty of foliage as background or they are lost against the daylight coming from behind them. Bear in mind also that most flowers in church are seen from a distance and so arrangements need to be bold.

Don't limit yourself to flowers. Different colours and textures of foliage can make a magnificent display, and so can single branches of blossom strategically placed. Fruit and vegetables are as decorative as flowers and are especially appropriate if you are getting married in the country in an agricultural community. Arrangements of colourful fruit and vegetables like shiny red and green apples, grapes, hops, miniature (or full size) pineapples, peppers of every colour, aubergines, bunches of tiny carrots with their frothy greenery attached, ornamental cabbage, orange gourds and leeks look magnificent on flat surfaces like window sills.

Be prepared to counter the argument that it looks like a harvest-festival celebration – if it is actually harvest-festival time, displays of produce are entirely appropriate, and at other times they continue the long tradition of tying in weddings with the farming calendar. A certain amount of produce, in conjunction with flowers, adds emphasis to the fertility-celebration aspect of marriage and would be especially appropriate if you and your fiancé hope to have a large family or already have children from previous marriages and are being blessed in church.

There are superstitions attached to flowers as there are to almost all aspects of weddings which you can happily ignore if you want. Lilac, for example, is supposed to have a funereal association, since the tree often dies when another lilac tree in the same garden is cut down. If you are superstitious you can take note of such ideas, but most brides are sanguine about them and don't let them inhibit their plans for the day. Lilac is an exceptionally beautiful flower with its proud cones of colour on elegant stalks with neat, well-shaped leaves, and it has a heavenly scent. It will look beautiful among your wedding flowers, so if you like it, use it. The Christian church has adapted many pagan ideas over the centuries and overridden others – you will be continuing the trend.

Before deciding where you want your flowers, take a slow walk around the church, noting the position and suitability of special features like the font. Pew ends are a popular position for small flower arrangements, but be careful if the aisle is quite narrow or you plan to wear a dress with a wide, sweeping skirt. Your florist should be able to supply supports for the pew-end arrangements. If you want to fill the font with flowers, check with the minister that there isn't a christening the next day for which the flowers would cause a problem.

Your church or place of worship is where you and your fiancé will actually become husband and wife – it is a serious occasion of great importance as well as a joyful one. Most people like to express the significance and joy by decorating the building with flowers, foliage and fruit, whose beauty and colours bring the place to life. Don't feel you have to make extravagant gestures, though these can be stunning. A few perfect blooms or fruit can be just as effective.

The obvious position for flowers in church is the altar – either placed on top, or to one or both sides of it. Free-standing arrangements are useful in positions where there isn't a window sill or other prop to support the flowers. They also have the advantage of being tall so there is no danger of the flowers being hidden when the congregation stands during the actual marriage ceremony and the hymns. This is a consideration when you plan all the church flower arrangements, not just free-standing ones.

FLOWERS FOR THE RECEPTION

It may be only an hour or two between the arrival of the first guests at the church and your departure from it as a married woman, but your guests will be sitting quietly, concentrating on their surroundings and the service. The reception afterwards is likely to last a lot longer but your guests will be eating, drinking and talking. In general, however, as much attention is given to flowers at the party location as to flowers in church, the main difference being that these will be seen close up whereas in church they are mostly seen at a distance. The colour theme begun in church can be continued, and also the mood of the wedding, whether it is sophisticated elegance or country simplicity.

If the reception is to be held in your parents' home or another private house, flowers must be in keeping with the style and colours of the rooms. Lilies and roses would be more at home than stocks and sweet peas in a grandly decorated room with polished antique furniture. The same applies to some extent in hotels, though the decorations here are usually more neutral than in private homes where the taste of one person has been paramount.

The posts down the middle of a marquee are ideal for flower arrangements which will make an impact. Make sure the impact isn't physical by fixing the flowers sufficiently high up. The sides of a marquee usually descend quite low and aren't ideal for anything but small flower arrangements, perhaps beneath the light brackets. A buffet is enlivened by flowers and foliage and so are the tables at which you and your guests sit to eat. High or top table, where you and your husband and parents will sit, can be marked by special flowers or, if it is a long narrow table at which you will be sitting on one side only, by swags of flowers and foliage along the side your guests will see. If you are serving finger food, a spray of herbs and flowers on each dish will make the food even more appetising.

Use pot plants as well as cut flowers – daisy trees, white

Food and drink are even more enticing when decorated with flowers, fruit and foliage, whether on a buffet or on individual tables.

hydrangeas, cyclamen, lilies, primulas and bulbs like tulips and daffodils in spring – placed strategically in passages, cloakrooms, entrances, unused fireplaces or to bar the doors of private rooms not to be used by guests. You and your family can enjoy these long after the cut flowers have wilted and they make welcome presents for kind helpers who have enabled the wedding day to run smoothly. The dais or place where the speeches will be made is a key spot for flowers, and so is the cake itself and the table on which it stands.

As in church, remember that foliage, fruit and vegetables can make as great a decorative impact as flowers. Pyramids of rosy apples enliven window sills; baskets of glossy plums and grapes, or oranges and lemons, brighten up dark corners of a house or marquee (even better if the fruit is mixed with leaves); ivy trails romantically from picture frames and across mantelpieces; swags of laurel with wedding bows in white or your theme colour draw attention to important doorways. Seasonal vegetables will also continue the theme of fertility and fruitfulness that has been linked with wedding celebrations over the centuries and in every culture.

At the beginning, as people fill the reception room and become animated in their conversations with each other, the atmosphere will become warmer, drawing out the sweetness of scented flowers. At the end of the reception, when you leave for your honeymoon, you may be loath to part with your beautiful bouquet by throwing it to your bridesmaids or sisters. Don't feel obliged to – this is a recent custom and primarily American rather than English. If you want to throw something, use your floral head-dress or a posy of flowers similar to your bouquet, made specially for the purpose. Then you can take your bouquet with you on honeymoon, or for the first night if you are subsequently going abroad, to remind you of your wedding day.

6
CELEBRATIONS

LETTERS OF CONGRATULATION

Once you have become engaged, and certainly once the announcement of your forthcoming marriage has appeared in the newspapers, you will receive letters and notes of congratulation. Relations and friends from far and wide, some of them almost forgotten after years in which you have seen or heard from them only rarely, will want to wish you joy and find out something about your husband-to-be and your new life. You may also be given some engagement presents. Receiving these letters and presents is one of the most enjoyable parts of early engagement, but they do require an answer and thanks. In fact, from the moment that your engagement is public knowledge until months after your wedding, you will be writing notes and letters almost continuously. Keeping up with your correspondence may seem a chore, but it would be rude of you to ignore the people who have written to you and who give you presents either now or later, when the wedding approaches. Of course, you are grateful for the present and the thought behind it, and the giver wants to know that it reached you safely.

There is a charming tradition that an engaged man is congratulated upon his engagement, but a woman is offered best wishes for her future. To offer her congratulations would be to suggest she had been involved in a chase and had got her man. The man is presumed to be the lucky one so he gets the congratulations. Older people, especially, follow this code and will write to say, 'Very best wishes on your engagement . . . I hope you will be very happy together!' rather than 'Congratulations! What fantastic news', which is how your contemporaries may put it. The feelings are the same; engagement is a time of hope and optimism for the future, and people find happiness attractive and want to be involved.

Whether or not you enjoy the business of putting pen to paper, it is worth being prepared. In practical terms this means being equipped before your engagement is announced with a large stock of stamps and stationery, including fibre-tip or ink pens rather than scratchy disposable ballpoints, and matching paper and envelopes. If you have writing paper and correspondence cards printed with your address you will find them invaluable and labour saving. You also need to have a system prepared. Where will you put the letters when they arrive, for your fiancé to see? Where will you keep the letters to be answered, and where the ones that have been answered?

In order to keep track of whom you have replied to, either keep a list with their names and the date you wrote back, or write the date on the letter itself, or both. Engagement presents should be entered in the front of your wedding-present book so you need to get this organised (see page 170). If you can put together a compact correspondence kit, with small quantities of stationery and stamps and the latest letters and cards received, you will find your task much easier because you will be able to write a quick letter wherever you find yourself – on a train, in the dentist's waiting-room or in your lunch hour at work.

There are certain facts which your correspondents will be eager to know:

▶ Something about your fiancé: what he does and how long you have known him, for example

▶ When you are getting married and where

▶ Where you will live

▶ How your marriage will affect your lives – you or he may have to change job so that you can live in the same town, for example, or you plan to return to his home country in a year or two, or he's a keen skiier so you will be taking up the sport

These demands may seem impertinent or trivial, but once your engagement is announced you must think of yourselves as public property to a certain extent. A marriage is a public event, and in any case you want people to know and love your fiancé as you do. Once you are married you can get on with being private people again.

You don't need to go into much detail, and your reply also gives you an opportunity to pave the way for an invitation or the lack of an invitation to the wedding. If the person who has written is a relative or close friend, give them the date of the wedding so that they don't accept another invitation for that day. Only do this with a few intimates – your personal invitation list is almost certain to be shorter than you would like and a reply to a letter does not signify an automatic invitation. For anyone else, simply mention the season, 'early next spring', or the month and, if you are planning quite a small wedding, say so. This will introduce the idea that numbers are going to be limited.

An example of a reply to a letter of congratulation on your marriage is:

Dear Paul,

Thank you so much for your letter and your good wishes. It was lovely to hear from you after so long. I don't feel we have lost touch as I hear about your exploits fairly frequently from Aunt Mabel.

George is a doctor in a country practice in Gloucestershire so we will be living in his cottage a few doors down from the surgery after our honeymoon. I can continue my business there, working from home, but I shall have to get some new headed paper! The wedding is planned for August 12th and I do hope you will be able to come.

Give us a ring if you are ever down here. Thanks again for writing.

With love from

Louisa

Don't let the backlog of letters get you down. If you find letter-writing really painful, look upon this as good practice. Don't agonise over your replies and do bear in mind the pleasure you will be giving the people to whom you are writing.

THE WEDDING LIST

Here is a list of special presents to give you ideas of your own:

Cast-iron enamelled cookware including large casserole pans; other big pans and dishes for when you have a family or give parties

Wok, steamer, chicken brick or other less than obvious cooking utensil

Electric citrus-fruit juicer

Decanters

Glass jugs. These are invaluable and almost bound to get broken. Store a couple away as replacements

Crystal glasses. Even if you only use them a few times a year they are a joy to have and are likely to get broken over the years, so suggest more than you think you will ever need

Kitchen aprons and oven gloves. The best aprons start high, reach low, have long strings you can cross at the back and tie in front, a big pocket and are made of heavy absorbent material. Oven gloves should cover and protect your wrists and be lined with heat resistant material

Large glass storage jars with airtight stoppers

Pepper and salt mills

Huge heavy wooden chopping board and carving board

A set of spongeware mugs with your initial on one, your future husband's on another, the best man's on another, etc. to remind you of your wedding.

Set of ever-sharp, dishwasher-proof kitchen knives in a wooden block

Picnic hamper and good-quality picnic ware such as plastic plates and glasses, vacuum flasks and cold box

Rectangular basket with divisions to hold bottles secure

Folding picnic rug made from warm wool with detachable rubber backing sheet

Folding wooden boot tree

Folding canvas and wood garden chairs

Barbeque and equipment such as long-handled tongs and fold-over wire mesh grip

Garden tools

Heat-resistant table mats

Trays. Small round ones for dressing-tables or a few cups of coffee. A hand-painted one for display and special occasions. A clear plastic one which goes with every type of interior and furniture. All heat resistant

Heat-resistant cover for your beautiful dining-table, to go under a tablecloth

Machine-washable tablecloths

Real linen table napkins

Real linen pillowcases. There is nothing like the feel and absorbency of real linen under your face at night. Because they are rectangular they are easy to iron

Tapestry cushions, perhaps antique ones

Antique boxes and small pictures; decorative plates for hanging on the wall rather than eating off

Print of the church where you are to be married, or some other significant place like the place your fiancé proposed, or showing the flowers and fruit of the month in which you will be married

Telephones

Telephone answering machine

Best-quality power tools

Toolbox

Rechargeable torch

Classic anglepoise reading (or work) lamp

Visitors' book or address book embossed with your names or initials or the date of your wedding

Photograph frames

Leather-bound photograph album

Reference books such as: world atlas, road atlas, large dictionary, general encyclopaedia, encyclopaedia of antiques or DIY or plants or cookery, complete works of Shakespeare

Small bookshelves. You never have enough and you can store all sorts of things other than books on them

Wall-hanging mirror

Decorative row of hand-painted wooden or metal hooks or pegs

GIFTS

Your friends and family will want to celebrate your marriage by giving you presents for your new life and in particular your home. They are not obliged to give you a gift because you have invited them to your wedding, but most will want to. Some people will have a clear idea of what they want to give but most will be grateful for advice. The ideal form of guidance is the wedding list.

THE WEDDING LIST

Having a list of suggested gifts at a department store is a custom which has been practised for generations and has been found to be so successful for everyone concerned that an increasing number of shops offer the service. The shop clearly benefits from the sales, and should offer a thorough service in return. Ask about details such as

free delivery, special orders, written information about who has given you what and the return of duplicated goods. The shop may have a set time-scale – your list may be available to donors for only three months before your wedding and one month afterwards, for example.

If you and your fiancé have almost everything practical necessary for your home, you might decide to place your list with a specialist shop rather than a general department store. Many people have two lists – one in each of their home towns if these are far apart, or one in a department store and one in

a specialist kitchen or linen shop. This gives your friends and relatives a larger choice of possible gifts which is always sensible as they may find that an item you requested was out of stock.

Shops vary in their methods of compiling your list. Some will send someone round with you to take note of the stock number of each item; other very busy ones will give you a chart of suggested types of item with boxes where you fill out the stock numbers yourselves. Whatever the method, be sure that you include suggested gifts from every price bracket, including things which cost just a few pounds.

CHOICE AND STYLE

It is important for you and your fiancé to have an idea of what you are going to put on your list before you visit the store. A busy shop floor is not the place to have a heated discussion about the relative merits of one type of frying pan or design of duvet cover over another. You will leave cross and exhausted and not at all sure that the things on your list are what you want.

There will be basic practical considerations: calculating what gadgets and technical equipment you actually need; matching the things you already have; ensuring that linen is machine washable and fits the beds and that cookware fits into the oven; checking that the china is dishwasher- and microwave-proof. Work these out as much as possible in advance, and take measurements with you (of your bed and your oven, for example). Before you go you should also have a clear idea of how you want your home to look. What style of bed linen and china and glass do you both like? This may be a matter of give and take or you may discover your tastes are easily compatible. If in doubt choose simple designs rather than elaborate ones, and if your tastes are identical and you trust each other to make the right choices, only one of you needs to compile the list.

IDEAS

A problem which many couples encounter is that they have had their own separate homes or a home together for some years and feel they already have all the pots and pans, sheets and towels, and every other practical thing they could ever need. You can't ask for money, even towards a good cause like your honeymoon or a new car, yet you know your family and friends would like some guidance as to what to give you.

The answer is to think ahead, and think bigger and better than ever before. You've always bought things on a budget; now think in terms of top quality you couldn't afford previously. You may have everything you need for a one- or two-bedroomed flat, but what if you have several children and move to a bigger house? You may have a lovely set of six crystal glasses which you bring out for dinner parties but what if you one day have a dining-table that seats ten, by which time only three of your goblets have remained unbroken? The drill you bought at a car-boot sale may have served you very well for a few years, but what about the rest of your life?

Thinking along these lines doesn't mean that everything on your list has to be expensive. On the contrary, some of the things you might put away to be used in five or ten years' time are easily affordable. You can also ask for a set of something, such as a dinner service, which your friends can buy in individual pieces rather than as a whole. You could have a short list but with the items of best quality and in sufficient quantity to last you many years.

LETTING PEOPLE KNOW

There's no point having a wedding list if nobody knows about it. Friends and relations are bound to ask your and your fiancé's parents, brothers and sisters and the best man whether you have a list and where it is. Your fiancé's family, and indeed yours, may live far away from the town where your wedding-list shop is and might welcome some information. If you type up a sheet of details and give the key people copies, they can pass this on to anyone asking about your list.

Information to include is:
► The name of the shop
► Its telephone number
► Its address including the post code
► Opening hours including weekends and any half days
► Telephone-order hours if different from opening hours
► A short résumé of the type of thing on your list at the shop
► The name of the wedding-list department for telephone enquiries (different stores call it different names)
► Forms of payment accepted, the name a cheque should be made out to and any other details of payment and delivery

If you have lists at more than one store give details for each on the same sheet

HOME-BASED LISTS

An alternative to a shop list is a home-based list. You make a list of the items you would welcome as presents, including as much specific information as you like (model number, capacity, colour, etc.) and photocopy it. You or some other person (your mother perhaps) keeps a master copy and sends photocopies to anyone who asks. They in turn cross off the present they have chosen and return it to you. You cross the item off any further copies of the list before distributing them.

This type of gift list is a far less convenient method of helping your friends give you a present that you really want. They have to go and choose, pay for, transport and wrap the gift in person, whereas the whole transaction can be done on the telephone with an in-store list. It is also difficult and tedious for the person keeping the master list.

KEEPING A RECORD

In the months between your engagement and your wedding you may receive presents almost every day, both from your wedding-list stores and from individuals. Shops do sometimes make mistakes in what they send you, and even without this it is easy to lose track of who has given you exactly what, when it arrived and whether and when you wrote to thank the donors. Keeping a detailed record from the start will help you be organised, and you will have the information at your fingertips if any dispute or misunderstanding arises. The book will also make a fascinating document for your grandchildren to read.

You will need:
► A book with lined or blank pages or a loose-leaf binder with a supply of file paper
► A packet of self-adhesive numbers, obtained from a good stationer
► Paper glue or double-sided adhesive tape for sticking cards in the book

Leave plenty of space for the information about each gift rather than cramming it in. Write the number of each present clearly, perhaps in a box, for easy reference. As each parcel arrives and is unpacked, stick the self-adhesive number to it to correspond with the number in the book. Cards with special messages can be stuck into the book too.

A comprehensive record will include:
▶ The name of the donor or donors
▶ A description of the gift including its brand, size, and model name and/or number
▶ Whether it is from your wedding list and the name of the shop
▶ The date you received it
▶ Where you received it
▶ Any comments about its condition
▶ The date you wrote to say thank you
▶ The address to which you wrote

Cheques need an extra entry: what you spent them on.

SAYING THANK YOU

You and your fiancé should share the task of writing thank-you letters. He could perhaps write to his family and friends about their presents and you to yours, or vice versa. You should write a short note even if you have thanked the donor in person when receiving it. Tell them how attractive/useful you think it is (be even more specific if you can), or if you cannot do that with any honesty, say something true about it. 'I've never seen anything quite like it', or 'the pattern is most intriguing', or 'it would look most striking in a room decorated in blue and white' are tactful remarks to make. If a gift is from a few people who have clubbed together, write to thank each individually; but if it came from a large group of people, your colleagues at work perhaps, write a single letter and give it to the most senior. Make it clear that it is addressed to everybody who contributed and be prepared to see it pinned on the noticeboard.

When writing to say thank-you for a cheque, tell the donor what you plan to spend it on. If you have no idea as yet, or if you hope to add several cheques together to buy one larger item, say so. Ideally you should write again when the thing has been bought, saying how useful or beautiful it is. If the manufacturers produce a brochure, get an extra one of these to send to the donor of the cheque.

Try not to get too far behind with your letters or you may find the thought of them depresses you. It is better to write a brief note promptly than a long letter months after the gift was received. Headed writing paper will make letter writing quicker (see page 166 for other helpful ideas).

UNWELCOME AND DUPLICATE GIFTS

The ideal is to avoid receiving unwelcome and duplicate gifts in the first place. A wedding list in an accessible store which also takes telephone orders is more likely to prevent them than a home-based list. If you do receive a duplicate gift and you know which shop it came from, exchange it. Write to thank the donor for the original gift. The alternative to exchanging it is putting it away for a future year, when the one you already have may be worn out or broken.

Avoiding unwelcome gifts is harder. One approach is to spread the message that there are certain things you would rather not be given, by word of mouth, starting with your parents and your fiancé's. You could also add a tactful note at the bottom of your wedding-list information sheet saying something along the lines of: 'P.S. There are certain things which Harry and Catherine are lucky enough to have plenty of already, including *pictures, ornaments, lamps, glass bowls* and *silver.*' Then you simply have to hope that the people who might have given you these things see and read the sheet or hear by word of mouth. It is almost certain, however, that you won't escape being given a few things you have specifically listed as prefer-nots.

Some of your presents are likely to be from people who you are fond of and for whose gift you are grateful but whose taste is totally different to yours. Their gift may seem to you to be hideous beyond belief, or completely useless. If it is shop-bought but you cannot exchange it because you don't know which shop it came from, you can hide it or give it to a charity after a suitable pause. If you can sell it some time after your wedding without the donor knowing, use the money to buy something you do like or need. Three years is a period after which your conscience should be able to rest easy. However, if you have been given an object which has been owned and treasured by the donor you should try to keep it rather than sell it. You might find that it turns out to be useful after all, or that your taste changes and after a while you become quite fond of it.

PRESENTS FOR ATTENDANTS

It is customary for the bridegroom to give each of the bride's attendants a present. These gifts need be neither grand nor extravagant: they are given simply to thank your attendants for helping to make your wedding day one of the happiest days of your lives. Though they are paid for and in theory given by your fiancé, he may not do anything more than write and sign the tags – which you have chosen and presented to him to complete. If you want your bridesmaids and pages to be sure of getting presents, you may have to find and choose them, wrap them and present them yourself.

BRIDESMAIDS

The traditional present for a bridesmaid is a small piece of jewellery – an expanding silver bangle engraved on the inside with the date of the wedding and the name or initials of the bridesmaid, a brooch or necklace or pair of ear rings made from pearl or coral, or a silver locket. The simplest approach is to give all the bridesmaids the same present, but you could scour your local antique shop or market for individual pieces of antique jewellery or small objects like figurines, scent bottles or boxes.

An enamel box decorated with the words 'Thank you', the name of the bridesmaid and the date of the wedding, or your and your fiancé's Christian names and the date, is an individual and attractive present. Photograph frames are always welcome (for pageboys too), and so are handkerchiefs – you could give each bridesmaid an Irish linen handkerchiefs with their initial hand-embroidered on the corner. Gifts which would be suitable for attendants of either sex are framed prints and drawings – a view of the church where you are being married, for example, or of a landscape in the locality – and books such as the Bible, *Oxford English Dictionary*, an anthology of love poems or a fine art book.

PRESENTS FOR SMALL CHILDREN

Adult and teenage bridesmaids are quite easy to choose presents for. Problems arise with small children. You can give them something special which they will be able to use or enjoy when they are older, but they will be too young to appreciate it now and may even lose it in the confusion at the reception. You could give them each a toy or something they can enjoy immediately, but this may not really be what you would like them to remember your wedding by. One solution is to do both – give a small, colourful toy for the day, well wrapped in colourful paper so opening the package is fun, and deliver the special present safely into the hands of their parents.

PAGEBOYS

Presents for girls are generally considered easier to find than suitable gifts for boys. The classic presents for pageboys are a fountain or rollerball pen or cufflinks. A pen is a suitable present for a bridesmaid too. Tankards also make good presents for boys – pewter or crystal is handsome and both can be engraved with initials, a name or names and the date of the wedding. A leather stud box with the boy's initials embossed in gold, or a tie pin, are other possibilities.

As with girls, a hunt through your local antique shops or market might throw up the ideal present, and if you are giving the bridesmaids decorated enamel boxes there is no reason why the boys could not have these too. You could either give them all the same design or choose different ones for your pages and bridesmaids, or a different design for each attendant according to their interests.

WHEN DO YOU GIVE THEM?

The presents can be given either before the service or at the reception. If you are giving them each a small piece of jewellery which you would like them to wear for the service, you can give them their parcels when you are all getting dressed. Otherwise, your fiancé can distribute them himself at the reception.

BEST MAN AND USHERS

If he wishes, your fiancé can also give his best man and the ushers presents. A blotter or bound notebook makes a suitable present, and so does a glass tankard, a keyring or a fine lawn handkerchief. Any of the books suggested for attendants would be welcome, as would any of the other gifts listed above, such as a photograph frame or a pen. Your best man and ushers will be delighted with whatever you decide to give them to remind them of your wedding day and the part they played.

THE WEDDING RECEPTION

WHERE TO HOLD THE RECEPTION

Where you hold your reception depends firstly upon a list of considerations such as how many people are invited and secondly upon the choice of possible locations near where your wedding is to take place. Make a list of each and compare your requirements with available locations.

Considerations include:
▶ How many guests
▶ Type of celebration:
    drinks and finger food
    buffet meal
    sit-down meal
    evening dance
▶ Size of your parents' home and garden
▶ Its accessibility and facilities
▶ Costs at alternative venues
▶ Time of year and part of the country

Possible locations:
▶ Your or your parents' home
▶ Marquee in your parents' or other private garden
▶ Large private premises lent for the occasion
▶ Club or clubhouse
▶ Village or church hall
▶ School or other institutional hall or dining-room
▶ Hotel
▶ Marquee in hotel garden
▶ Restaurant

Unusual wedding reception locations:
▶ Boat on canal or river
▶ Museum
▶ Theatre
▶ Stately home available for function hire
▶ Botanical glasshouse
▶ Agricultural buildings
▶ Zoo

If you hire a building (or vehicle) not regularly let for functions, check details like fire and licensing regulations with the owner/administrator and if necessary the local council. Get any assurances from the venue in writing, perhaps in their letter of confirmation. For a reception in your own home, take account of the following: security; fire escapes and fire-fighting equipment; insurance; contingency plans in case of exceptionally bad weather; coats; lavatories.

If you hire a marquee and don't want a couple of hundred people tramping into the house, consider hiring a cabin with portable loos. These can be perfectly pleasant, with chemical lavatories and moisturised hand wipes so that there is no need for a water supply for lavatories and hand basins. Quality does vary, so it is a good idea to inspect the cabin before hiring it.

If you are planning to hold your reception in a hotel or other commercial building, ask for estimates for a variety of different menus and types of drink from several establishments so that you can compare value for money. Check on financial details like tax, insurance, service charge and tips, as well as details of what is included in the price – for instance, equipment, flowers, candles, microphones, lighting and heating, linen and staffing. This applies equally to outside caterers, whom you should also ask about transport costs.

DECORATIONS

Hotels and other premises for hire may or may not allow you to arrange your own decorations (probably not, in view of fire regulations). Village, church and school halls are likely to be bare in appearance but may allow you more freedom to festoon the place with swags of foliage and flowers, balloons, white paper bows and streamers and even banners, in order to make the place look festive and give it a personal touch. Ask about decorations, including table flower arrangements, when you do your initial research into possible reception locations.

MORNING AND AFTERNOON

A morning wedding usually finishes at about lunchtime and is followed by a meal rather than just drinks and finger food. If this is too expensive, it would be better to have the wedding ceremony later, in the early afternoon, followed by a stand-up reception and tea. This is the simplest type of party following a wedding. However, if your guests have travelled a long distance, and in certain parts of the country, like the north of England, this might be considered an insubstantial celebration, depending on the quality and quantity of food you provide and whether or not the reception is being followed by an evening meal and dance.

If your wedding takes place in the late afternoon the party following it could consist of an early supper and dancing. In this way your guests are saved the trouble of going away to change for the evening party, and the celebrations will finish sufficiently early for guests who live a certain distance away to reach home at a reasonable hour. Whenever the meal is, it is courteous to invite the minister who married you to say grace or a blessing before the eating begins.

RECEIVING

The receiving line is the traditional way of welcoming your guests and giving them all the opportunity of greeting the bride and groom and their parents. Your friends and family can be introduced to your husband and his parents if they haven't already met them, and vice versa. The order in which you stand is: bride's mother, bride's father, groom's mother, groom's father, bride, groom. Your chief bridesmaid and attendants can join the receiving line if you and they wish it, although the custom has all but fallen into disuse.

At many weddings the full receiving line is dispensed with altogether. A mid-way arrangement is for the bride and groom alone to greet the guests. This is quicker than a full receiving line and appropriate if you and your husband are older, independent people. But some guests may never discover and speak to your and his parents. A wedding is a family occasion and guests usually appreciate a full receiving line. It can proceed from right to left or left to right, depending on the layout of the room.

Give some thought to your guests before they reach the receiving line. If you line up at the door of the room, will they be forced to queue for a long time in a narrow draughty hall or even outdoors in winter? The sensible place to form the receiving line is well into the room. Guests can then enter the room and mingle before joining the queue at a moment when it is conveniently short.

HIGH TABLE

At a reception party where you sit to eat, one table is reserved for you and your husband and both sets of parents. High or top table may be long, rectangular and set at one end or side of the room, or it may be the same shape as all the other tables and in amongst them. If it is the former, you will all sit along one side where you can see your guests and they can see you. This doesn't make for much communication or conversation between those seated at high table, but it is a popular arrangement because it is traditional.

The traditional seating order for high table is shown below (see seating plan A).

Difficulties can arise when parents are divorced and remarried or attached (see seating plan B), or when there are other complications. Only so many people can sit at high table yet everyone's feelings must be considered. Don't forget that the most important feelings are yours. If you don't get on with your father's wife or girlfriend, she can be an honoured guest and sit at the head of a nearby table with a close relation to escort her, but she does not have to sit at high table, even if your father is paying for the wedding. Strictly speaking, she is not part of the 'bridal party' which consists of you and your husband, your and his natural or adopted parents, the best man and the bridesmaids and pageboys. There is usually not room for all of these at high table, so there is certainly not room for stepparents or escorts unless you particularly want them.

If you are close to your stepparents and want to include them, you may have to reorganise the seating or arrange to have a

A		T A B L E	B
BEST MAN	T		CHIEF BRIDESMAID
GROOM'S MOTHER			BRIDE'S STEPFATHER
BRIDE'S FATHER	A		GROOM'S STEPMOTHER
BRIDE			GROOM'S FATHER
GROOM	B		BRIDE'S MOTHER
BRIDE'S MOTHER			GROOM
GROOM'S FATHER	L		BRIDE
CHIEF BRIDESMAID			BRIDE'S FATHER
	E		GROOM'S MOTHER
			GROOM'S STEPFATHER
			BRIDE'S STEPMOTHER
			BEST MAN

larger table. All attendants except the chief bridesmaid and the best man could sit at other tables to make room.

To include your stepparents, seat your stepmother on the best man's left and your stepfather on the chief bridesmaid's right. If you have been given away by someone other than your father, he sits at your left. If your mother gave you away, a brother or other close relation can sit at your left, or the person making the first toast, or your father-in-law. The basic seating plan can be adapted to your family circumstances in any way you wish, with your and your fiancé's blood relations usually included rather than more recent additions to your extended families.

SEATING YOUR GUESTS

Some people view the task of drawing up a seating plan as a chore to be avoided, while others relish the prospect of putting people together who have interests in common but have never met. This is certainly a more productive attitude. You yourselves will not have the opportunity of making all the introductions you would like, and people tend to stick to those they already know if they are not thrown together by a seating plan. It is not necessary to specify particular places at the table if you don't want to – simply allocate people to tables and leave them to seat themselves. You can either mix the generations or keep most tables of one age-group or another, but you should certainly try to mix your family and friends with your husband's. This is a rare opportunity for them to get to know each other en masse and is half the point of having

a party after the wedding ceremony.

Place a number, letter or name on each table, written clearly on a large card which can easily be seen by people searching for their places. List the names of the guests below each table title, on sheets of paper near the entrance. Pin these as high up as possible so that they can more easily be seen.

Before making your seating plan consider whether or not you are going to seat the professionals among your guests – your dressmaker, musicians, the photographer, video cameraman and sound technicians, for example. You could allocate them a table to themselves – a good idea in practi-

cal terms as they may each have to leap up from time to time to continue with their work – or arrange refreshments for them in another room.

Children can either be seated with their parents or at a table of their own, perhaps a low one with small chairs, depending on their ages and confidence. Consult their parents informally at an early stage to find out the children's own preferences.

MASTER OF CEREMONIES

Whether or not you have a master of ceremonies or toast master is entirely a matter of taste. If you have a receiving line he will ask each guest his name as he arrives at the head of the queue and announce it to your parents. He announces the meal, the cutting of the cake and the names of the speakers. He should also keep an eye on arrangements at the reception and help events proceed smoothly. If you don't have a master of ceremonies, the family and the best man cover these duties between them. Hotels and catering companies often have their own master of ceremonies and there are also freelancers who may be retired sergeant-majors or people who have completed an accredited course.

MUSIC AND ENTERTAINMENT

Music performed during a reception is easily overwhelmed by the sound of conversation. Guests raise their voices to be heard over the music, however beautiful it is. Some types of band such as a brass, jazz or steel band and instruments such as the bagpipes can hold their own. A string quartet or cocktail pianist is unlikely to be heard unless carefully amplified.

An alternative to seated musicians is a soloist or small group who can play while walking among the guests – an accordionist, guitarist or folk band for example. Establish the flexibility, time-wise, of any performers you consider. It is almost impossible to specify exactly when a reception party will start and end. Better to engage them for a set amount of time: three or four half-hour sessions, for example, with rest breaks in between (discuss the length of these). Decide whether you will offer the musicians refreshments in their breaks, and whether these will include alcoholic drink.

Small attendants and other children at the reception may understandably become bored and restless during the speeches and afterwards. Ideally, someone should be responsible for entertaining them in another room, keeping them busy and happy. One task they will enjoy is decorating the going-away car, blowing up balloons and tying old tin cans to the back bumper. Some thought needs to be given, in advance of the wedding, to supplying the necessary materials.

PRESENTS

Many guests will bring their gifts with them to the wedding, so a table needs to be provided at the reception in a convenient position where they can deposit them safely. The presents need to be secure during the reception and afterwards, possibly overnight, and someone such as the best man should be responsible for gathering them up in due course and delivering them to you or your parents afterwards.

COATS AND LOOS

In a hotel or on premises regularly let for functions, cloakroom arrangements will already be established. Find out the extent, security, appearance and any additional cost of these when doing initial research. On private premises – in your or someone else's home – and at a church, village or school hall or dining-room, it may be necessary to make distinctive signs with arrows saying 'COATS', 'LADIES',

'GENTLEMEN' and 'PARTY' to guide your guests in the right direction, both to and from cloakrooms and lavatories.

EVENING PARTIES

The cost of a marquee, which is considerable, becomes more worthwhile if you are having an evening dance as well as a lunchtime or afternoon reception. If you are exceptionally lucky you might even be able to share some of the cost with a neighbour who is celebrating an important birthday or wedding anniversary the next day. The disadvantage of having an evening party in a marquee is possible aggravation over noise. However much trouble you take to warn your immediate neighbours and the police, someone is almost certain to complain and the police are required to take complaints seriously. You shouldn't have this problem if your home is in rural surroundings.

If there is a gap between the reception and evening party you should make it large enough to allow your guests to go back to their hotels or wherever they are staying, rest and refresh themselves, have a bath and change before returning.

The people invited to the evening party do not have to be exactly the same as those who attended the wedding and reception. The emphasis could instead be on the young. Elderly relatives and your parents' friends could give way to your and your fiancé's friends, some of whom could not be invited to the wedding for lack of space. Invitations are issued separately for the wedding and evening party, so it is a simple matter to have two separate guest lists.

DANCING

An evening party is usually a dance with either a band or a disco, although there may be other entertainment as well. If you have a disco, discuss in detail the type of music you want at your party when researching possible disco companies. If you want the disco to play waltzes and Scottish reels in between classic sixties pop and the company representative poo-poos the idea, go to another disco company.

More formal types of dancing, such as waltzes and reels, are colourful alternatives. You can dance with a wider range of partners and everyone knows what is expected of them. For the same reason, a jazz or reeling band can be more successful for a

wedding than a pop band. Family of all ages can join in the dancing. A disco can be too loud to allow conversation – discuss this problem with companies when doing your research – whereas a jazz or reeling band is not usually so deafening that it prohibits conversation among people sitting at tables around the edge of the room. It also doesn't carry as far as the relentless beat of a disco.

OTHER ENTERTAINMENT

Entertainment in addition to a band or disco for dancing could consist of:
Comic cabaret
Family cabaret of songs and sketches
Magician
Fireworks

Acrobats or jugglers
Regimental Band
Whatever you choose, plan the entertainment well in advance and establish exactly what technical and other assistance any professional performers require (the same applies to a band or disco). Get these and a detailed financial agreement in writing. The best way to find a performer is to see their act at another event. If you find them any other way, such as by word of mouth or through their advertisement in the press, you must see them perform in front of an audience before you book them. Fireworks can be very dangerous so remember that the credentials and experience of a firework 'designer' should always be meticulously followed up.

After the solemnisation of a marriage, the reception is the time for noise and laughter, eating and drinking, celebrating life in general and your marriage in particular. You and your husband's family and friends have a chance to mingle and meet each other. The room where the reception is being held is festively decorated with flowers and bows.

Tables laid for a meal are made to look welcoming while the guests are entertained by musicians and dancers, or simply by the fun of seeing so many friends and relatives at such a joyful occasion. If you have a sit-down meal, a seating plan made in advance will help ensure that people who don't know each other but whom you think have something in common will actually meet; you will be too busy and distracted to make many introductions yourself.

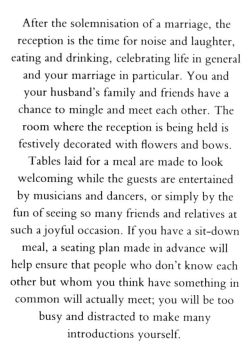

If you are lucky with the weather you may be able to hold your wedding reception outdoors. Don't count on it, however; have a suitable building or marquee prepared and look upon fine weather as an unexpected bonus. On a brilliant summer's day, sunshine and flowers and your guests' brightly-coloured clothes will shimmer like a moving kaleidoscope. When the time comes to cut the cake, speeches are made by an old friend of you and your family, by your husband and his best man. Most brides are relieved that they too do not have to make a speech; others have a particular message they wish to convey, or special thanks they wish to give, and choose to make a speech of their own. The main aim of all the speeches, apart from giving thanks to all the people who have helped, is to introduce you and your husband to the other's family.

CUTTING THE CAKE

Biscuits and cakes have been part of the wedding festivities for centuries, but the custom of the bride and groom together making the first cut in the huge iced cake is more recent. Icing on wedding cakes is supposed to have been introduced by chefs whom King Charles II brought back to England with him from exile in France, and by the middle of the nineteenth century the icing was sufficiently thick and hard (bearing the weight of many tiers) to require the efforts of both bride and groom in order to cut through it.

WHEN TO CUT THE CAKE

The cake can be cut at any time which suits your plan for the day. Often this is at the end of a meal or a stand-up reception. The bride and groom and the person making the first toast gather around the cake where it has been on display on a table, perhaps on a dais, and the best man or master of ceremonies announces that the cake is about to be cut. Everyone gathers round the dais (if they are not seated) and you and your husband together make the first incision. The bottom layers are whisked away as soon as this first, ceremonial, cut has been made and are cut into fingers in the kitchen. The ceremony of cutting the cake goes hand in hand with the speeches, which follow it. Pieces of cake are distributed among the guests once the speeches have finished, and thirst quenching cups of tea (or perhaps coffee, if the speeches are taking place at the end of a meal) are also on offer. The bride and groom then go and change into their going-away clothes before being sent off with a rousing farewell, and the day's festivities come to an end.

There is no reason why you cannot rearrange this order of events, especially if you are serving a sit-down meal or if you know that the best man and your husband would be grateful for the ordeal of making speeches to be over as quickly as possible so that they can start to enjoy themselves. The cake can be cut and speeches made before the meal but once everyone is seated. If your guests have not had anything to eat at this point, the cake cutting and speeches could take place after the first course has been served and removed. Those making speeches can relax a little if their audience is comfortably seated, fed and watered.

The cake cutting and speeches could take place at a stand-up reception as soon as the receiving line is completed. In this case the best man could add a few words when the speeches are over, to the effect that he hopes the guests won't rush away as the bride and groom are planning to remain some time before going to change. This would explain the situation to older friends and family who may otherwise assume proceedings are coming to a speedy close.

SWORDS AND KNIVES

Many families have a special sword or knife used for cutting the cake at weddings. Hotels and caterers usually supply a silver cutting implement as part of their overall package, but check that there is no extra charge for this when doing your research. If the implement you plan to use is unwieldy, a cut can be made in the cake before it is iced, and then iced over with a small decoration to indicate where it is. Your husband's regimental dress sword can then glide smoothly through the cake instead of causing an undignified struggle. Whatever you use to make the first cut, your task will be easier if you insert the point of the implement downwards first, before lowering the rest of the blade.

LEFT The wedding cake is usually cut immediately before the speeches and the bottom layer removed to be divided into pieces for your guests.

LEFT Your wedding cake can be made to any recipe – carrot or chocolate are by no means unknown.

THE CAKE

THE RECIPE

Sweetmeats, fruits and grains, with their connotations of fertility and harvest, have been associated with weddings at least since the Greeks threw them over the bride and groom rather like confetti. Today in Britain a rich fruit cake finished with layers of almond paste and snowy white icing is thought traditional at weddings, but you can have any type of cake you want. A steep mountain of profiteroles, glazed with caramelised sugar and called a croquembouche, is the usual wedding cake in other parts of Europe, and you would not be alone in choosing a chocolate or even a carrot cake as your wedding cake.

The most delicious rich fruit cakes are made a couple of months before the wedding and steeped in extra alcohol for a few weeks after that, so you need to begin your cake research almost as soon as you become engaged. You may plan to order your cake from a bakery or an individual, in which case ask for a small one to try at home (give your parents some too) to make sure you like their recipe. Ingredients usually include currants, raisins, sultanas, glacé cherries, mixed peel, blanched almonds, lemon rind, plain flour, cinnamon, mixed spices, butter, brown sugar, treacle and eggs. If you want a variation on their usual recipe, discuss this with them in detail and write it in your letter of confirmation. Repeat your requirement when you confirm on the telephone at about the time they should be making the cake (two months before your wedding). If you have asked for something out of the ordinary, they may think, 'She can't really mean that!' and go ahead with whatever they think appropriate, unless you remind them that you can and *do* really mean that.

DECORATIONS

Look at photographs of previous cakes decorated by the shops or people who may make yours. Bear in mind that it would probably be unwise to ask them to do something completely new, unless

The traditional recipe for wedding cake is rich and fruity. The most usual wedding cake is round or square, has several layers and is iced in white and decorated with ribbons and flowers.

they are top professionals and you can provide them with a picture (such as a photograph from a magazine or book) of what you want. An alternative to elaborate coloured icing decorations is plain white, and another is fresh flowers between each tier as well as on the top. Discuss this with your florist. She will need to know the number of tiers, their sizes, the number of pillars supporting each tier and the sort of arrangements you have in mind. Flowers and greenery filling the gap between each tier and tumbling over the edges look very pretty, although you don't want the cake itself to disappear into a thicket.

Consider what you would like on the very top of the cake. An arrangement of fresh flowers in a small silver vase is probably the most sophisticated and tasteful. A bride and groom under an arch or with a miniature church in the background is an entertaining alternative as is a yacht if your and your husband's passion is sailing, or a model of your new home. These can be made for you in coloured icing by a specialist cake shop. Take a photograph to show them exactly what you want.

SIZE AND SHAPE

Your cake can be any shape you want – round, square, hexagonal (six sides), octagonal (eight sides), heart shaped, or even shaped into your and your fiancé's initials. The only limitation is finding someone to make the cake, but a little research should reveal a willing baker or cake-maker. You should also bear in mind the number of your guests. One of the reasons why the rich fruit cake continues to be so popular could be that it goes a long way. A lighter recipe may be easier to make into special shapes but you will need more of it to satisfy a couple of hundred enthusiastic friends and relations. The answer is to have a more elaborate cake of your choice but also to have a traditional round or – even more practical – square, iced cake in the background to be cut up for the guests. This can be a good idea whatever your shape of cake, if you have more than about 150 guests, as it would take a great many layers to feed them and you may in any case want to keep the top one for a christening.

If you intend sending pieces of cake (see page 186) to absent friends, remember to include these people in the calculations about the total sizes and weights of cake you need.

QUANTITIES

As a guide to quantity, an 11-inch round cake feeds roughly 80 people, a 9-inch roughly 50 and a 6-inch roughly 25. This is assuming that your guests have already had other things to eat and don't want doorstep slices. The depth of the cake is also significant. Your bakery or cake-maker should give you an estimate of quantity based on their experience of their recipe and depth of cake.

Don't forget that cake is heavy and you don't want the pillars supporting one layer to sink into the lower one. If you are worried about the strength and hardness of your icing, you could place a thin cake board, smaller in diameter than the cake but wide enough to support the pillars, on top of each layer of cake. Alternatively, you could do away with pillars altogether and place the cake on an 'S'-shaped stand of the type now available.

MAKING IT YOURSELF

If you or a parent or sibling is an experienced cook or, even better, an expert baker, you could consider making the cake yourselves. This is a useful economy, leaving you a little more money to spend on other things. The fruit cake can be iced by someone other than yourself – in fact it *should* be iced by someone else if none of you is expert and confident, or at least practised. The cake is a prominent feature at a wedding reception and, although many errors can be covered up with ribbon around the sides of the tiers and decoration and flowers on top of each layer, you don't want to be worrying that the icing is going to be a disaster. The final icing should not be done more than a couple of days before the cake is eaten.

A reliable cook book, one which is either devoted to celebration cakes or written by one of the gurus of cookery (for example Delia Smith), will have a detailed recipe for rich fruit cake and a chart giving quantities of ingredients for different sizes of round and square cake. It should also give you advice on making and applying almond paste, icing and decorations. Make a small version before finally deciding on a recipe, to check that you like the flavour and that the recipe's instructions are accurate.

POSTING IT

If you want to send absent friends and relations a piece of your wedding cake, buy the boxes well in advance of the wedding and have some cake cut to fit them. Arrange for someone reliable to post them immediately after the wedding.

The cake is a focus of attention at the reception, for people of all ages, especially children who may not have seen anything quite like it before.

There are no rules about the size and shape of your cake. It can be round, square, any geometric shape, heart-shaped, or in the form of your initials. It can be as many or as few layers as you like, sitting on each other or raised up on pillars or a stand, and its decoration can follow the theme of your wedding in terms of colour and style. At a winter wedding, wreaths of holly with red berries, all made from icing, can decorate an otherwise traditional snowy white cake.

Chocolate is a popular alternative to a fruit cake and other possibilities are walnut cake, carrot cake or zingy orange and lemon cake.

SPEECHES

WHEN TO MAKE THEM

The speeches are made after you and your husband have made the ceremonial first cut in your wedding cake. The length of speeches depends on various factors. Is the audience standing up or comfortably seated? If the latter, the speeches can afford to be slightly longer; if the former, they need to be short. Are the speakers experienced and witty, or nervous novices? Give them strict instructions in advance to be brief if the latter, or if you fear their speeches may be dull. If the former, suggest a time limit but do not make it too constricting as a well-performed speech is a pleasure to hear and will contribute hugely to the success of your reception and the enjoyment of your guests. You also need to let the speakers know whether or not there is to be a microphone.

The best man or master of ceremonies announces the first speaker by saying something along the lines of: 'Ladies and gentlemen, please be silent for Mr Henry Allingham who will propose the toast of the bride and groom.'

THE FIRST TOAST

This is made by a relation or close friend of the bride's family. The speech and toast are usually made by a man of your parents' generation but can equally well be made by a female relation or family friend, or by a relative who is contemporary with you rather than your parents. Often it is the bride's father who gives the guests a sketch of her character and achievements to date before proposing the health of the newly-married couple. By all means ask your father if he would like to do this, but be prepared for him to refuse. Many fathers feel they have enough to cope with without speechmaking. In addition, you may be grateful if he has nothing on his mind on your wedding day and can be your free-lance troubleshooter.

One of the points of a wedding reception is for members of the two families to get some idea who this person is that you or your husband has married. These introductions need to be clear and factual as well as suitably enthusiastic about their subjects. If the person making the first toast doesn't take the initiative beforehand you should suggest to him or her that it would be a good idea for you to have a talk. Make sure he has the facts about your life right; if you are a good sport you might supply him with one or two stories which are funny at your own expense.

The first speech should not last longer than five or ten minutes, after which the speaker lifts his glass and says something like: 'Now I would ask you all to raise your glasses and wish Sophie and Michael long life, health and every happiness in the future. Sophie and Michael.' Everyone present stands up (if not already standing) as he speaks and joins in to toast the couple by name. If the speech was good the guests may applaud, but they are not required to do so.

THE GROOM'S SPEECH

The groom can either speak without introduction, or wait to be introduced by either the best man or the master of ceremonies. He and the best man should remember that they are addressing people of all age groups, not just their own. In-jokes should be avoided, and the speeches should be carefully written and rehearsed in advance, out loud, so that nerves do not cause either man to wander from the point.

Of the three speeches, the groom's is superficially the easiest but often diplomatically the most difficult. He usually begins with a compliment to you, and goes on to thank your parents for having brought you up and allowed you to marry him. He also thanks them, or the people who are the hosts, for the splendid reception (and party if there is to be one in the evening). If a divorced parent of yours who is not acting as host, or his own parents, have made a financial contribution or a contribution in kind, this is the moment to acknowledge that if you want to. 'Special thanks are also due to Sophie's father who has so kindly contributed the champagne', or, if he wants to be less specific: '. . . Sophie's father, without whose help this splendid reception would not be what it is . . .'. Any feathers previously ruffled in a family with complications caused by divorces and remarriages can be smoothed over in the course of the groom's speech. He needs to be well briefed, however, and you and he have to have decided exactly how he is going to word any tricky acknowledgements.

A pleasant part of his speech involves thanking your guests for coming, particularly those who have travelled a considerable distance and those who have come from abroad or in the face of adversity. He also thanks everyone for their generous and wonderfully useful gifts.

Your husband need not say more, but often there is a list of people who have given really special help in making the wedding such an occasion and whom you would like to thank publicly. If the flowers are exceptionally beautiful or the food was made by your aunt, your guests will be interested to know this.

The groom ends by thanking his best man for his support and toasting the bridesmaids and pages, whom he may mention by name or not as he likes. Everyone raises their glasses and joins in the toast.

THE BEST MAN'S SPEECH

The best man replies on behalf of the bridesmaids, thanking the groom for his toast. He then gives a sketch of the man you have just married, for the benefit of your family and friends. There is no need for him to try to be funny, especially if there is any chance of his humour falling flat. He should certainly avoid any stories, such as tales about previous girlfriends, which are in poor taste. The best man's speech ends with another toast to you and your husband.

TELEGRAMS

At this point, or before his final toast, the best man may read out any interesting telegrams (strictly speaking called telemessages) which absent friends and family have sent you. The messages themselves are not usually of great originality or interest to anyone but you. Ideally he should simply read out the name of the senders and the place from which the telegram has been sent. You can take the messages away with you to read later, or they can be waiting for your return, or you can even sit down and read them during the reception. Decide in advance what you want to do and make sure someone takes responsibility for keeping them safe.

A BRIDE'S SPEECH

Traditionally the bride does not make a speech, and you may be glad of this. However, brides increasingly wish to speak on their own behalf, especially when they have something specific to say. If you have married a man who has children from a previous marriage, or if you have children of your own, this would be a good opportunity to thank them for making you (or your husband) welcome, and voicing your hopes that you will be a good friend to them in the future (or your husband to your children).

There are often other personal reasons for a bride making a short speech. If your sister is going to be married soon, you may wish to draw everyone's attention to this and wish her well, or you may want to congratulate your parents on a special wedding anniversary or thank them for their hard work in making the garden look so beautiful for your wedding day. Your wedding is a family event and any family message is appropriate, even more so if it is connected with your marriage. Discuss what you want to say with your fiancé before the wedding so that he does not steal your thunder or duplicate your thanks.

Decide also when you wish to make your speech. You could speak before your husband, or after him, or even after the best man. Better earlier, so that what you have to say does not come over as an afterthought.

OTHER SPEECHES

In some countries it is the custom for many members of your and your husband's family to stand and make a short speech and toast, but in general three or four speeches are enough. If anyone other than the four people whose speeches are described above wishes to speak they should consult you beforehand (or be asked well in advance) and instructed to be very brief. If your guests are standing, think seriously about allowing any further speeches. The audience may not be in the mood for listening any longer.

FOOD

A wedding would hardly be a wedding without the feast that follows. In some Mediterranean countries the carousing continues for days and nights, giving rise to the classic tale of the great-uncle who dies of a heart attack in the excitement of the first hours and isn't discovered for a week because that is how long the party lasts. Song and dance and much consumption of food and drink is the natural consequence of people's desire to celebrate the joys of life in general and in particular to mark your passing from one stage in your life to the next.

In purely practical terms, your guests need to be sustained. Some may have travelled for many hours or even days and it would be inconsiderate to wave them off without so much as a cheese sandwich. You will need food too, although you may find that your mental state is such that hunger doesn't make much impression on you. And in any case you will want to have a few words with your friends and family, and a meal is the ideal occasion.

The main, perhaps the only, constraint on what you serve is money. If you have a large budget you can give your guests canapés before a splendid meal of three or more courses, cooked and cleared up by professionals behind the scenes and served by a team of starched waiters and waitresses. Most people have a fairly strict budget and have to choose options within it in terms of type and choice of food and method of service. On a tight budget you can either serve just canapés or slightly more substantial finger food at a stand-up reception in a relatively inexpensive location, or cook the food yourself.

CANAPÉS

Even if you are giving your guests a meal which they will sit down to eat, you won't want to rush into the meal but will want some time beforehand in which to greet them and exchange a few words. Drinks will be served, and you might like to have small cold canapés for them to eat before lunch or supper proper. These could be in lieu of a first course, so that when you sit down you go straight into the main course, or in addition to it. They want to be small in size and attractively presented, whetting the appetite for what is to follow. You can either circulate dishes of one or two types only, or you can arrange dishes with several different types of canapés and leave these around the place for people to help themselves. In the latter case you need fewer people circulating food, but the stationary dishes do need to be checked and replenished regularly.

Some delicious examples of canapés:

▶ Triangles or spirals of smoked salmon and brown bread
▶ Pickled herring on black bread
▶ Avocado mousse in pastry boats
▶ Asparagus tips wrapped in brown bread or prosciutto
▶ Crudités (raw vegetables such as cucumber, carrot and celery cut into sticks) with dips such as blue cheese, spicy tomato, or mustard or garlic mayonnaise
▶ Cheese straws
▶ Cheese or herb cream profiteroles
▶ Small discs of bread, or round biscuits, with a slice of hard-boiled egg topped with a piece of anchovy
▶ Tiny brown-bread sandwiches or bridge rolls filled with kipper pâté or cucumber and ground pepper
▶ Hard-boiled quails' eggs with spicy salt and pepper
▶ Cubes of melon wrapped in Parma ham
▶ Heart-shaped croutons with chicken-liver pâté
▶ Heart-shaped cucumber cut-outs with herby cream cheese

FINGER FOOD

This is in lieu of a meal and consists of small savouries and some more substantial bite-sized or larger pieces of food, some of which can be served hot.

Some ideas for finger food:
▶ Miniature egg flans such as quiche lorraine or smoked trout (hot or cold)
▶ Cheese-pastry tartlets filled with lightly cooked vegetables in mayonnaise (cold)

- ▶ Chicken or beef satay with peanut-sauce dip (hot, cold dip)
- ▶ Vegetable samosas (hot or cold)
- ▶ Miniature blinis: pancake with sour cream and caviar or lumpfish roe (cold)
- ▶ Devils on horseback: prunes wrapped in bacon (hot)
- ▶ Filo-pastry parcels containing spinach and cheese or spicy chicken (hot or cold)
- ▶ Miniature spring rolls (hot)
- ▶ Prawn and sesame toasts (hot)
- ▶ Miniature pizzas (hot)
- ▶ Gougons of sole or monkfish in breadcrumbs (hot)
- ▶ Thin pastry cups filled with seafood and salad or light fish or chicken curry (cold)
- ▶ Cherry tomatoes stuffed with herby or curried cream cheese (cold)

The fillings should be home-made rather than mass produced. There is no comparison, for example, between real and shop-bought mayonnaise or pâté. If you are not confident about making pastry, however, you could allow yourself to buy it – time is better spent on the contents. Many types, including filo, can now be bought in most reputable supermarkets.

BUFFETS

Your guests can either stand to eat, in which case everything must be in small enough pieces to be easily eaten with a fork only, or sit down. They can either sit at tables or places allocated according to a seating plan, or sit anywhere they wish. The buffet can be manned with people who

will serve your guests or with only a few people to keep it tidy and replenish the dishes or replace them with fresh ones.

The two problems which arise with buffets are queues and under-use, and both can be avoided. Queues happen when everyone descends on the buffet at the same time. This can be avoided, if your guests are seated according to a plan, by inviting them to the buffet table by table. Someone clearly needs to be appointed to do this, and the system needs to be explained briefly to your guests before the meal begins.

Under-use occurs when the choice of dishes is repeated once or more along a long buffet but the guests queue from one end only. This can also be avoided, by placing the repeat dishes on a separate table at a different place in the room, or by

explaining to the guests before the meal begins that they can be served from the buffet at intervals along it, not from one end only. The key is communication. If you write or print the menu on a card on each table, your guests have a chance to read and decide which dishes they would like before arriving at the buffet, which will also help to speed things up.

Keep the choice of dishes at a buffet simple so that guests can see what there is and so that the buffet itself does not look a mess. Decorate it with flowers and foliage to make it look fresh and colourful.

SIT-DOWN MEALS

A meal at which your guests are seated can either be served at the table (needing at least one waiter or waitress per ten people) or from a buffet. The first course can be on the table when the guests arrive. All the arguments in favour of having a seating plan (see pages 176-177) are reasons supporting having a sit-down meal. Cost is the usual limitation, but with determination, hard work, good planning and ingenuity, this can be overcome.

CHILDREN

Children are notoriously fussy about food, and the joys of the most exquisite poached salmon with hollandaise sauce is likely to be lost on them. The simplest approach is to take a quick informal poll of their parents to find out what their favourite food is. If fish fingers and baked beans come out on top, don't have any qualms about serving them with these, at a table of their own.

SPECIAL DIETS

Many people have special diets for religious or medical reasons. If you know what these dietary requirements are, bear them in mind and ensure there is something these friends and relations can eat and enjoy, but don't let it rule your menu. In addition, an ever increasing number of people are vegetarian or non-meat eating. If you or your family is vegetarian or non-meat eating, you should not feel you must serve meat for the sake of your guests (the same applies to alcoholic drink if you are teetotal). This is an opportunity to show just how colourful, varied and delicious meat-free and vegetarian food really is.

COOKING YOURSELF

Cooking the food yourself, with the help of reliable friends and relations, is a way of having a feast at greatly reduced cost. The cost in terms of your energy is obviously far greater, however, and must not be underestimated. You need to think like a general. For your lunch and supper to be a success you need to be more thorough and well organised than you have ever been before. You must accept every offer of help (unless you know the person is unreliable or unsuitable) and not be afraid to ask for help too. At the same time, remember that many apparently organised people are actually hopelessly vague and un-businesslike, however willing they are, when it comes to doing something within a budget and a deadline. You should begin by doubling any estimates they give as to time and money involved in their achieving anything. When you ask for help, always give the person a real choice rather than making them feel they must help because you have asked. You don't want them to drop out at the last minute.

As well as people you will probably need to borrow freezer space and equipment. Make a generous estimate of the amount of both that you will need in the run-up to your wedding and secure the loans as soon as possible. You need to keep a meticulous record of all loans, made when, by whom, and for what period, as well as drawing up a logistics chart. This will show who is to fetch and carry every item, from where, to where, when, and who is to take it back and when. Discuss insurance with every person who lends you things and if theirs does not cover the occasion make sure yours does.

When it comes to perishables like food and flowers, be absolutely clear about what you are paying for and which things other people have offered to donate. Think also about who is to serve and clear, and what is to be done with leftovers, if there are any. Make sure someone takes responsibility for the wedding day itself and the time you are on honeymoon – you don't want to be distracted by culinary and organisational matters.

The timetable of cooking, freezing, defrosting, preparing and serving food needs to be detailed. Quantities need to be worked out and recipes tested. By the end of the experience you will feel like an experienced caterer. But the food itself need not be complicated; in fact, it is much better to keep it simple and to be imagina-

tive with colours and flavours. Cold roast chicken with a choice of hot curry sauce or cold herb mayonnaise, served with new potatoes in their skins (hot or cold) sprinkled with chives, and two or three interesting salads, followed by some fruit-based puddings is a feast for summer. In winter you can serve cold food so long as the room and the guests are warm. Alternatively you could serve a hot casserole with hot rice and cold salads, but only if you can borrow or hire the equipment to keep the casserole and rice hot. Don't serve hot food if you cannot keep it hot and avoid hot vegetables as they become tired when kept warm.

Spend some time in your local or county library equipping yourself with recipes and information about freezing and defrosting. Don't hesitate to ask the advice of anyone you know who has catered for a wedding or big party in the past.

HOTELS AND CATERERS

A reliable hotel or caterer will lift the burden of catering from your shoulders, but only after you have done sound research and are absolutely satisfied with the style and quality of their work and the financial arrangements, down to the smallest detail such as the cost of cloakroom staff, table napkins and the provision of a cake stand and knife. Ask about anything you don't understand and be suspicious of anyone who tries to intimidate you with technical terms or their knowledgeable air. You can always go elsewhere. Good hotels and caterers, like everyone connected with weddings, do get booked up quickly, especially for summer weddings, so do your research and remember to make your bookings as soon as possible after you have become engaged.

DRINK

CHAMPAGNE

The classic drink for a wedding, champagne has become greatly more expensive since the producers revised their prices towards the end of the 1980s. There is nothing quite like it, however. Its dry crispness and the tingle of bubbles on your tongue are thrilling and completely in tune with the excitement engendered by an occasion like a wedding.

Champagne comes in three qualities. Non-vintage, which is dry (or Brut) and is a blend of wines from a number of different years, designed so that it always tastes the same. This is the least expensive. Vintage champagne is made in particularly good years, from that year's crop of grapes only. More expensive, it is generally heavier and richer than non-vintage champagne. De luxe champagnes are prestigious blends or vintages which are very expensive and more suited to an intimate dinner for two than a wedding. There is also pink or rosé champagne.

A reputable wine dealer will help you choose champagne and other drink, and if you buy it all from him he should give you a decent discount and may provide glasses as well. Own label champagne and other wine can be perfectly drinkable and good value. Arrange for him to take back unopened cases, but don't count on there being too many of these. Returning them may also affect your discount, so it may be more worthwhile to keep any leftover champagne for special occasions over the next year or so.

Allow at least two glasses of champagne per person if you are going to serve it only on arrival and with the cake, at least four glasses for the whole reception counting six glasses per bottle. Don't underestimate the amount of champagne and other drink you will need – unless you want to risk running out. Chill it to about 5°C (40°F) – if you are at home do this in a bath with a half and half mixture of ice and water.

If your reception is at a hotel or restaurant, or if you are employing a caterer, go into the question of drink in detail with them. As part of a package including food as well, champagne and other drink may be affordably priced. But often the mark-up which hotels, restaurants and caterers impose is such (100 per cent is not uncommon) that it is cheaper to pay corkage for their staff to open and pour the bottles, while buying your own supplies elsewhere.

SPARKLING WINE

There are some excellent sparkling wines available – better tasting in fact than some champagne – so don't dismiss this as an alternative to serving champagne. It is less expensive and just as celebratory. Good sparkling wines are produced in the same way as champagne; others have simply had carbon-dioxide bubbles pumped into them. The second-fermentation champagne method is best for making dry sparkling wines but is much less important for sweet ones. Three reputable sparkling wines are Saumur (from a region on the Loire), Cremant d'Alsace and Cremant de Bourgogne, but not all sparkling wine is French. You could consider a wine from Spain, America, Australia or even India.

WINE

Allow at least half a bottle of wine per head. White wine seems to go down faster than red at wedding receptions – perhaps because white is nearer champagne in colour and flavour – at an estimated rate of two to one.

CUPS AND PUNCHES

The colour and delicious flavour of cold alcohol-based and non-alcoholic cups and punches make them an attractive alternative to straight champagne or wine, and ideal for a summer wedding celebration. Pimm's No. 1 is the best known and is rightly popular. Dilute it with half lemonade and half soda or sparkling water for a drier flavour and float generous quantities of sliced fruit such as oranges, apples and strawberries in it. You could concoct your own similar cup with equal quantities of gin, dry white vermouth and sweet red vermouth diluted to taste, but experiment with this first and make sure you like it as it is not identical to Pimm's.

A cup made from white wine, cider and soda (or sparkling water) is another refreshing summer drink with sparkle. Mix the three equally in a large jug with a good dash of brandy, cucumber and sprigs of fresh mint. As the afternoon progresses you could increase the proportion of soda to alcohol, especially if the day is hot.

Non-alcoholic punches can be made from fruit juices and sparkling water. One of the simplest mixtures is apple juice and soda with sprigs of fresh mint. A mixture of orange and grapefruit juice has a special tang, and apple and blackcurrant is good too. Give the mixtures time to chill before serving them, but don't let the ice melt completely and dilute the flavour.

OTHER ALCOHOLIC DRINKS

Dry sherry is a delicious drink whose image is unjustly burdened with ideas of gentility and elderly vicars. Serve it cold as an alternative to champagne when your guests arrive. Cocktails and spirits are more complicated and time consuming to serve than wines such as sherry and champagne, and consumption is also difficult to predict.

WATER AND SQUASH

Whatever else you serve, you should serve water. If you live in an area where tapwater tastes good, have a large jug of this with plenty of ice and slices of lemon in it on each table. If your guests are standing up, several waiters and waitresses can circulate with a jug in one hand and a bottle of mineral water or a jug of fruit juice in the other. People who are drinking water and soft drinks should be given tumblers – champagne tulips don't hold enough. At a sit-down meal, everyone should have a tumbler for water as well as a wine glass.

The choice of mineral waters, sparkling and still, is huge and you probably have a favourite. Serve this in quantity at your reception, and leave bottles of it on every table. You may be pleased by the drop in your drinks bill. Many people prefer non-alcoholic drink – alcohol is a drug after all – while some switch after a glass or two of champagne or wine, and others are driving and avoid alcohol for that reason. Plain lemon and orange squash is popular too, especially at a dance where people get hot and want something thirst quenching, and children will probably prefer this to fizzy water.

TEA, COFFEE AND TISANES

In summer, iced tea or coffee is refreshing at the end of a meal, but it is more usual to offer hot tea or coffee. Coffee has long been thought of as a fashionable drink, but many people now prefer tea and are also more discerning about its flavour than they once were. If you wouldn't consider offering your guests a cheap vinegary plonk as wine, you should likewise not expect them to enjoy a cheap blend of tea with no identifiable country or region of origin, however famous the brand name. Make the tea with freshly boiled water and don't let it stew with the leaves – remove them once the tea is a good colour.

An alternative to coffee or tea is a tisane – an infusion of the dried leaves and flowers of a herb such as camomile or mint. Tisanes are generally caffeine-free and have a fresh flavour which clears the palate and the head at the end of a hearty meal.

GLASSES

Tall tumbler	*Short tumbler*	*V-shaped glass*	*Goblet*	*Wine glass*	*Champagne flute*
An invaluable glass for non-alcoholic drinks as it does not need refilling as often as a short tumbler. Place on the tables at a sit-down meal for your guests to drink iced mineral water from.	If you serve mixed drinks as your guests arrive, short tumblers are suitable for whisky, gin and tonic and other spirits.	Only really suitable for cocktails. If your reception is at a hotel or restaurant there may be a barman who would make cocktails for your guests but you need to establish this in advance.	Generous in size, a goblet is deep and broad with a short stem and base sufficiently wide to take its weight. Ideal for mixed cups and punches like Pimm's in summer. If unavailable use tall tumblers.	A wine glass is what it says: a glass for drinking wine. Don't serve non-alcoholic drinks in wine glasses – they don't hold enough and the drinker will be annoyed by constantly having to ask for more.	This, rather than a saucer-shaped glass, is correct for champagne. The saucer lets the bubbles escape quickly while the flute retains them and the scent of the wine for longer.

7
AFTER THE WEDDING

GOING AWAY

The moment when you leave to go on honeymoon is exciting and bemusing. For months you have been planning and arranging, concerned with every detail of your wedding and thinking about it constantly. All day you have been surrounded by the warmth and noise of your and your fiancé's family and friends. Suddenly it's over. Now, as you draw away from the waving crowd, cheering and shouting their good wishes, there are just the two of you alone together – you and your husband. For the first time since you were married you will have a chance to be quiet together and begin to relax and take in the day's momentous events. You may look at each other in amazement to think that at last it has actually happened. You really are married to each other, after so much waiting, and this is the beginning of your married life. It is too much to take in at once, and you don't need to rush. You have the days of your honeymoon in which to wind down and think about your new life.

There are three aspects to your going away which you have to plan: when to go, how to travel, and what to wear. You want to leave before your guests but you don't want to rush away too early and cut the party short. It's fun to travel in an unusual form of transport (joining your own car around the corner) but may be simpler and more practical to use your own from the start. And you both want to be smart but comfortable. As with every detail of your wedding, the choice comes down to matters of practicality, taste and cost.

When you go depends on the format of your wedding day. At a late morning or early afternoon wedding followed by a

stand-up reception, you go away in the afternoon after the cake has been cut and speeches made, and once you feel you've had a chance to say at least a few words to all your guests. If there is a dance in the evening, you go away from the reception after the cake cutting and speeches in your going-away clothes, and return later (you in your wedding dress and your husband in evening dress such as black tie), leaving the party quietly at an appropriate moment. If your reception is in the later afternoon and followed immediately by dancing, you stay for some of the dancing but leave in time for your older guests to see you off and get home (or get back to their hotels) before they collapse with exhaustion. Ten o'clock or half past is not too late.

The simplest and most obvious vehicle

to travel in is your or your husband's car. If you use his it is one less thing for you to have to think about. He is responsible for making sure it is spotlessly clean, inside and out, it works and has petrol, oil and windscreen-washing fluid. He and the best man should ensure it has both your honeymoon luggage (the best man can liaise with your chief bridesmaid or mother about your luggage). Even if you go away from the reception in some other vehicle, you will need your own car (and your luggage) at some point, either just around the corner or at the hotel where you will spend your first night. Your husband and his best man should arrange for the car to be in the right place the day before your wedding day or in good time on the day. All you and your husband will need to take with you when you go away is a small holdall, containing your spongebag and anything else you needed when preparing on the day for your wedding.

If you don't want to go away in your or your husband's car then there are many interesting alternatives such as: antique or veteran car, black cab, red London bus, motorbike, pedal bikes or a tandem, pony and trap or coach and horses, horseback, elephant, farm tractor, boat, helicopter, aeroplane, hot-air balloon (see page 59 for further suggestions). If someone you know owns one of these you could ask to hire it – they may offer you the use of it as a wedding present – and if you or your husband or a parent has one of these as a hobby or for work your choice is all but made. Have a contingency plan, however, as the weather cannot be predicted, and neither can illness on the part of a pilot or animal.

One advantage of going away in something other than your own car is that the latter may escape being decorated with balloons, loo paper, spray-on writing, old shoes and cans, and other messy matter which you will probably want to remove, out of sight of your guests, before continuing on your journey.

What you wear depends on how you are travelling, but the usual attire for going away is smart and colourful. You could wear a suit or dress and a hat; your husband wears a suit and colourful tie. You and he could each have something specially made for the occasion, or you could buy a new outfit, or wear something from your wardrobe. Getting married is a good excuse for reviewing your appearance and investing in a new, smart outfit. Most brides find they are able to wear their going-away outfit on countless occasions including other people's weddings, and that because of this the initial cost works out at good value as a result.

When you change, you can either do so together or you can each have someone to help. You in particular may need your chief bridesmaid or sister or mother to help you out of your wedding dress and hang it up safely. Someone should be appointed to take your small luggage to the going-away vehicle before you yourselves emerge. You don't want to be struggling with numerous holdalls and carrier bags as your guests wave you off.

At a winter wedding you can wear luxurious heavy fabrics such as velvet, wool and fake fur in rich, strong colours. In spring and autumn, wear light wool which will keep you warm, and have a coat and umbrella to hand just in case. In summer, linen and silk are light but strong, and colours can be brilliant or pale and subtle. Shoes should be leather and coloured or dark for peace of mind – fabrics and pale colours are riskier as they tend to show marks more easily. Your hat, bag and shoes can match or be different colours to match the colours of your suit or dress. If you can manage to arrange it without him knowing what you will be wearing, your husband's tie, socks and even handkerchief can match or correspond with the colours of your outfit.

The easiest vehicle to go away in is your or your husband's own car, but other vehicles are fun. An antique or veteran car, a bicycle or motorbike, a horse or tractor, a helicopter or aeroplane . . . if you can organise it, why not indulge yourselves?

FIRST NIGHT

When you wake up, the morning after your wedding, you will wonder if you are dreaming. Did it really happen? Are we really married? It did and you are, and you will be ready for a hearty breakfast to begin your first whole day as a married couple. You will enjoy it all the more if your surroundings are comfortable and convenient. The hotel where you spend your first night should be a refuge after the excitement and exhaustion of your wedding day, and a launching pad for your honeymoon.

Word of mouth is often the best recommendation when choosing a hotel, and the local telephone directories and tourist board should also be a help. When you make enquiries at various hotels near you, check the availability of a double room (with double beds) rather than a twin. You don't want to find that you can't cuddle up on your first night of marriage. Ask about honeymoon specials too – some hotels will give you a special room for the price of an ordinary one, or include a champagne breakfast. Make sure that you can have breakfast in your room, and that the final hour for serving breakfast isn't too early for you. Airport hotels are modern and can be rather 'international' and anonymous, but they often have 'honeymoon specials' for couples flying the next morning which can reduce the stress of travelling abroad. The atmosphere of the hotel where you stay is as important as the friendliness (but not familiarity) of the people running it, so you, your fiancé or your mother should go and see the shortlist of possible hotels in person and report back.

When you visit, explain that you are deciding where to spend the first night of your honeymoon and ask to see the rooms available (this is more likely to be possible if you visit midweek or off-season). Take a brochure and tariff away with you and make a note on it of your impressions. Once you have decided, ring to make your booking and remind them that it's the first night of your honeymoon – if they have an ounce of romance there will be special flowers awaiting your arrival.

If your reception is taking place at a hotel, you have the choice of staying there or elsewhere. The advantage of staying in the same place is convenience. A room for the night may also be part of an overall wedding package the hotel offers. A disadvantage is that you don't get away from your guests completely until you leave the next day.

KEEPING THE SECRET

You don't want to be antisocial or feel that you are in hiding, but on the other hand it is nice to know that once you have gone away and everyone has waved you off you really are alone together. To achieve this the hotel where you stay needs to have been kept a secret from your guests so that none of them stays there. This can be done, with a little planning. If there is a famous hotel near you and you don't particularly want to stay there yourselves, put it on the list of possible hotels which you enclose with guests' invitations. Include several other hotels on the list, from all price ranges, but leave out the one where you will be staying. Keep the number of people who know where you will be staying to an absolute minimum – no one need know except you and your fiancé and possibly your parents, if they have to make practical arrangements. The two (or four) of you must not tell anyone else. Once one other person knows, everyone will know. It is a matter of self-discipline, helped by not even referring to your first night in company so that speculation is kept to a minimum.

HONEYMOON

Your fiancé might want to organise your honeymoon without your knowing where you are going. Many brides' honeymoon ideal is still to be whisked away to a distant and exotic (or local and cosy) destination, metaphorically blindfolded. He needs to do his research thoroughly to be sure that you want to go where he does, and he needs to give you very specific instructions about the necessary innoculations, equipment and wardrobe in plenty of time for these to be arranged. Visas, insurance and local currency will have to be obtained by him alone together with all tickets. Of course, it need not be the groom who is the organiser and keeper of the secret – the bride can do it just as well if she has the time and inclination.

Even if you plan and book your honeymoon together, you might want to keep it a secret from your family and friends. This is very simple – you don't tell them until after your return. There is no reason to tell them if you don't want to. Most couples talk about their honeymoon when asked because they are excited about it and looking forward to it. Whether or not you keep it a secret is entirely up to you.

HONEYMOON TRAVEL

Deciding where to go for your honeymoon can be a baffling business. Your honeymoon is supposed to be the trip of a lifetime but there are so many destinations to choose from and so many types of holiday. A friend has just come back from an exotic faraway place and insists it is ideal for you, but you are saving up to furnish and decorate your new home. You dream of a cottage on a windswept Cornish or Scottish coast, long walks and log fires. Or you have dreamed since childhood of spending some time messing about in boats on the Norfolk Broads. On the other hand, if you don't go on a tropical trip now, when will you ever be able to afford the time and money?

There are several arguments in favour of the 'now or never' theory. The most powerful of these is children. If in the future you have them you may want your holidays to be times you devote to them after months of snatched evenings after work and all-too-short weekends. In addition, you may be acutely aware of the cost of clothing, feeding, housing and educating them. A trip up the Nile or a safari in Kenya suddenly seems like an unrealistic luxury, and a potentially unhappy one if it separates you from your beloved offspring for three or four weeks. Another convincing argument is that your employer or clients, and your fiancé's, are more likely to

Your honeymoon is a time to relax and recover from the excitement and hard work your wedding involved. Take time to wind down in whatever way suits you both best, and get used to being alone together, just the two of you. You belong to each other now.

be agreeable to your taking a large amount of holiday for a one-off honeymoon trip than for an ordinary summer holiday.

A honeymoon abroad need not be any more expensive than other summer holidays. There are package holidays to small hotels on Greek islands or large beach hotels in Spain to fit most holiday budgets. Read the brochures carefully and you may find a real gem – something that suits your tastes and pastimes as well as your pocket.

One of the disadvantages of a honeymoon abroad is the travelling. After the hard work of organising your wedding and the excitement of the day itself, the idea of six, ten or more hours spent travelling from door to door, before you can really relax again, may not appeal. Airports are not, in general, romantic places and charter flights can be delayed for hours in the busiest months. Trains, ferries and hovercrafts can be more fun and sometimes take no more time in total than flying, if your destination is not too far away on the Continent, in Ireland or Scandinavia. On the other hand, you may enjoy the travelling, especially if you aren't used to it. If travel abroad is something new, the novelty can override the boredom of queues and delays.

There is an increasing interest in domestic holidays. The British Isles have such a variety of beautiful landscapes, and few people can say they have seen it all. It is possible to stay not only in hotels, farmhouses and self-catering cottages all over the country, but there are also some unusual buildings of great beauty and architectural interest available for rental. In addition there is a new type of rented house or cottage, where the owners have a menu

from which you can order a home-cooked meal each day which they will put in your fridge in the early evening. You eat it when you want it. Thus some of the domestic work associated with cottage holidays is removed.

Rented cottages and houses have disadvantages and advantages for a honeymoon. There isn't room service or a laundry service, or a bar, and there is no grand diningroom to dress for and eat in at the end of the day. On the other hand, in a cottage there is no one to tell you when you can or can't eat meals and no one trying to clean your room when you want another few hours in bed – in fact you don't have to get up at all if you don't want to. Hotels can be officious and make some people nervous, but the best do offer discreetly efficient service and labour-free comfort.

Of course, you don't have to stay restfully in one place. Not everyone wants or needs to collapse with exhaustion on their honeymoon and independent travel will not necessarily wear you out. If you are adventurous or experienced travellers, you could go on a driving tour of a region of France or a cycling tour of Northumbrian monuments and churches. And you don't have to be alone – you could take a coach trip or opt for a learning holiday like sailing, photography or dry-stone walling. Don't be distracted from what you really want by the stereotype of the holiday on an island surrounded by blue sea and white sandy beaches. It doesn't suit everybody. Whatever holiday you choose and wherever you stay, book as far in advance as possible to be sure of getting exactly what you want.

Essential Honeymoon Travel Tips

Whether you have an open mind or have decided exactly where you want to go, you might appreciate the following alphabetical list of travellers' tips on what to take with you and what to do when you get to your honeymoon destination.

ALARM CLOCK Leave it at home. Your honeymoon is a time for lying in and lazing about, unless you have boundless energy and are naturally early risers in which case you won't need it anyway.

BICYCLES There's nothing like cycling for really experiencing the countryside. Explore country lanes and breathe in sweet hedgerow scents. Only for the fit and saddle-hardened, however.

BOATS According to Ratty, in *Wind in the Willows*, 'There is nothing half so much worth doing as simply messing about in boats . . .'. You could chug gently along Britain's canals in a gaily-painted narrow boat or charter a yacht for a tailor-made honeymoon cruise around the Greek islands or the 'fairy' coast of south-west Ireland.

BOOKS Take all those you've been meaning to read for months and never had the time to open along with: travel books about the country or region you are visiting and novels set in it: detailed guidebooks with the opening times of museums and where to find the best shops and restaurants. Finally a book of crosswords and something deliciously frivolous to relax your minds while your bodies lounge by the pool.

CAMERA Take one that does everything

for you so you can simply point and press. Your photographic record of your honeymoon may become one of your most treasured possessions.

CONTRACEPTION Don't forget to take yours with you if you would prefer not to start your marriage with an unplanned pregnancy.

DIET Eat the local cuisine when you are abroad and your experience of the country will be enriched, but take advice about the water before you go.

EYES which can get tired and red with travelling. Remove make-up (or keep it minimal) for long journeys with no opportunity to cleanse them properly. If you wear contact lenses take your fluids and a case in your hand luggage, and don't forget a spare pair of spectacles.

FILM Take several rolls with you as it is often more expensive abroad.

HAIR This is as vulnerable to the sun, cold and wind as your skin. Take a sunscreen conditioner if you are honeymooning in a hot, cold or windy country.

HATS They may be a nuisance to pack but they are vital in the sun. If you can't be bothered to pack any buy some locally when you get there.

INSURANCE Don't leave home without any. Check that you will be flown home in case of illness or emergency and insure for five times the amount in the USA that you would in Europe. Read your policy carefully to see exactly what is covered.

JET LAG Ways to avoid it include cutting out champagne and all other alcohol on the journey. Drink plenty of non-carbonated liquid to avoid dehydration.

LEGS Make an appointment for a few days before your wedding if you have them waxed. Otherwise, remember to take your wax strips or razor for legs as smooth as eggs.

LUGGAGE Think of the misery if it goes missing, so pack your hand luggage carefully, with your money, valuables, contraceptives, spongebag, swimsuit and a change of clothing.

MAKE-UP Take a small kit of essentials with you rather than the full works. Your husband loves you for yourself, not for your purple mascara.

MONEY Take most of this in the form of traveller's cheques for a worry-free honeymoon. Note the numbers and keep them in a safe place in case the cheques are stolen. Order your local currency from a bank or travel agent well in advance, taking enough to see you through the first day or two, and check whether you need to keep some aside to pay airport taxes on the way home. Alternatively, look into the possibility of using Eurocheques or getting cash through your credit card.

MOSQUITOES They can make life a misery for the fair-skinned or particularly tasty. Take plenty of reputable, easily-applied, non-greasy repellent and buy a burning coil when you get there.

NATURAL FABRICS In general, these are the most comfortable to wear for travelling. They are also the coolest and most comfortable to wear in hot climates as well as the warmest (though not necessarily most waterproof) in cold ones.

NOTEBOOK Don't forget one so you can record your impressions in writing and visually by collecting postcards, menus and labels.

ORIENT EXPRESS Why not travel abroad on this most romantic of trains which evokes memories of a previous age of bustling stations, puffing steam, and urgent whistles? The only drawback for honeymooners is that space does not allow for double bunks.

PACKING Do it the day before your wedding, and put all the heavy things at the bottom, followed by heavy separates, then dresses, and finally the things you will need first, such as night clothes and swimming things. Pack your camera, documents, valuables and washing things in your hand luggage if you are travelling abroad.

PASSPORT If you are planning to take your husband's name and want to change your passport accordingly, send it at least six weeks before your wedding to your nearest passport office in Liverpool, Newport, Peterborough, Glasgow, Belfast, or to the London Passport Office, Clive House, Petty France, London SW1H 9HD, with the three relevant forms completed and signed. These are: Form C (for altering a current passport): Forms PD2 and PD3 (undertakings from you and your minister or registrar that the passport will be returned if the marriage does not take place). You should get your passport back, post-

dated to your marriage, within five weeks. If your passport has run out or you have never had one, send Form A instead of Form C with two photographs. All forms are available at main post offices and passport offices. There is no legal requirement for you to change your name or your passport, and you could simply travel with your old one and take your marriage certificate with you to avoid any confusion.

PERIODS If yours threatens to coincide with your honeymoon, consult your doctor about continuing the pill right through two cycles. Or simply take a generous supply of your usual medication and tampons or towels. There's nothing wrong with sex during a period – the only drawbacks are that it can be a bit messy, depending on the heaviness of your usual flow, and cramps can make you feel anything but romantic.

POLITICS There is always political instability and upheaval somewhere in the world, sometimes resulting in violence and civil war. Before booking your honeymoon, check carefully that the place you want to go to is safe.

SKIN Remember this needs protection at all times. Always use a protective cream in the sun or wind, however weak the rays or breezes feel on your face. For a confidence-building tan before you go, apply a reputable fake colour in advance to parts which won't show on your wedding day, like your legs and body. Beware of sunburn – it has been linked to skin cancer and, anyway, a milky-white skin can be as beautiful as any tan. Use good-quality

barrier cream with a high protection factor (10 or more).

SKIRT If you visit churches or other religious buildings abroad, take a skirt as you may be refused entry in shorts.

SMALL You don't want to heave a suitcase full of half-empty full-size bottles of shampoo and skin products, so buy mini versions for your honeymoon.

SUNGLASSES You must have a good pair to protect your eyes from the harmful glare of the sun, snow, sea or sand. Ask an optician for advice and be prepared to pay more for a pair that will be really effective.

TRAVEL SICKNESS If you are prone to this, get a pharmacist to recommend, or a doctor to prescribe, medication. Alternatively try motion sickness bands which are now available from chemists and sailing shops. These are elasticated wrist bands with a hemispherical bump on the inside which you fit against a pressure point on the inside of your wrist.

VILLA For a really exclusive sunny holiday take a villa with a pool and staff to take the 'self' out of self-catering.

VISA Don't go without this if your honeymoon country requires one. Check with the travel agent and the country's embassy if in doubt, and submit your passports to a visa agency who (for a fee) will get the necessary visas for you.

WEDDINGS ABROAD Why not walk barefoot along a golden beach instead of neatly shod up the aisle? Combine your wedding and honeymoon, but make sure the paperwork is complete.

WEDDING ANNOUNCEMENTS

The custom of announcing a marriage in the newspapers has almost disappeared. Some parents remember that it was always done in their day and wish to do the same for their daughters but there are now rarely more than one or two such announcements, if any, in a national newspaper's court or gazette page on any one day. Some people consider such an announcement unnecessarily ostentatious, or an extravagance, and for these reasons if no others you should definitely not feel your wedding is incomplete without it. If you do decide to publish an announcement, the information should be delivered in writing or telephoned to the newspapers as soon as possible after the wedding has actually taken place. The bride's parents make the arrangements and pay so do check the charges first. A full and detailed announcement for the court or gazette page might read:

Mr George Brown
and Miss Catherine Smart
The marriage took place on Saturday at All Saints, Crossbridge, between Mr George Brown, only son of Mr Peter and Lady Alice Brown, of Rose Cottage, Pallington, and Miss Catherine Smart, younger daughter of Dr and Mrs Gareth Smart, of The Old Rectory, Crossbridge. The Rector, The Revd Patrick O'Malley, officiated.

The bride, who was given in marriage by her father, wore a gown of white ribbon lace and chiffon, and a silk veil held in place by white roses. She carried a spray of white and pink roses and lilies of the valley. Miss Elizabeth Smart, Miss Eunice Brown, Petronella Carter, Jane Carter, Harry Brown and Peter Wood attended her. Mr Philip Cross was best man. A reception was held at the home of the bride and the honeymoon will be spent in Scotland.

It is also possible for the announcement to appear in the paper's personal columns, in which case it will be shorter. An example is:

Farrell: Walker – On April 22nd, 1989, at the Church of St Michael and All Angels, Fambridge, Anthony Farrell to Helen Walker.

There are circumstances in which a couple might prefer to announce their marriage, after the event, rather than their engagement before it. They might have been living together for a long time and decided to marry quietly in church; the bride might be a widow and prefer a quiet wedding; or divorcees who have married in a register office might prefer to make their new status known in this way. In any of these cases the newspaper announcement could be similarly worded but brief:

Mr A. Stuart and
Mrs L.P. Gibbs
The marriage took place in Edinburgh on Saturday 30 June between Archibald Stuart, son of the late Mr and Mrs Alexander Stuart, and Lucy Gibbs, daughter of Mr and Mrs Edward Smith.

If you opt for a small or quiet wedding or are marrying abroad you can inform your friends, relations and work colleagues of your new status, name or address with a printed card to be sent out in the same way as a change of address card. This could be very plain, or colourful and decorated, and say:

William Jones and Fenella Abdy are now married and living at 24, Rosetti Avenue, Oxford OX9T 4PH, telephone 0298-49688.

Or, more informally:

James and Sheila Craddock wish to inform you that they were married on 30 May in Manchester and have moved into their new home at 54, Rose Lane, Ebdon, Lancashire, telephone 0892-49384, where they hope you will visit them soon.

An informal wedding announcement can be combined with a party invitation for your housewarming in your new home, with the usual details about the date, time and place of the celebration. If your wedding announcement is going to friends and family abroad, you could send them a copy of a good snapshot of the two of you on your wedding day.

SAYING THANK YOU

A wedding is an occasion that not only needs but positively attracts good will and helping hands. Of course you want to thank everyone who has contributed to the most wonderful day of your life, but what is the best way? One of three methods is bound to suit every 'thank you'. You can either offer your thanks in person, in writing, or with a present – a small token of your appreciation of what they have done.

IN PERSON

When you see the person who has contributed in some way, either by lending objects or by actually helping, you will of course say thank you. But is this enough? The answer is yes – be natural and sincere when you say thank you and the person should feel properly thanked. They will understand that they are just one of many who have helped and won't expect a letter.

In a few special cases, where the person has done something spectacular and visible, she or he can be thanked in your husband's or your speech. If your sister has iced the cake with exquisite icing roses and ribbons, or a friend has decorated the reception location with magnificent flower displays, your guests will be interested to be told this, briefly. You or your husband can offer them thanks and if your guests feel inclined and the results are particularly magnificent they may even applaud.

An exception is often the person who has conducted your marriage service. He or she usually does so for a fee, but in spite of this it is quite usual for the groom to offer thanks in his speech, because of the importance of the favour that the minister has done you. The person who married you and your husband will always be special to you both, unless something has gone positively wrong in your relationship with him, and many couples like to acknowledge this by thanking him publicly for his support and for making you man and wife. None of the celebrations would be possible without him, so your guests have reason to be grateful to him too.

IN WRITING

When you wish to thank someone who has contributed professional services for a fee, and who may or may not also be a personal or family friend or contact, it is more appropriate to do so briefly in writing. A card or note after the wedding is sufficient. If you aren't superstitious, you could even write these thank-yous before the wedding and send them after you return from your honeymoon, to save work later. Alternatively, buy some picture postcards while on honeymoon, and write and send them after you have returned. Don't burden yourself with thank-you writing while away.

WITH A PRESENT

When the person's contribution has been visual, the dressmaker or florist for example, you might like to send them a photograph which shows their work. It may be some weeks or even months before you get your photographs finally sorted out, so send a card in the meantime, thanking them and telling them that a photograph will follow. It could be either an official photograph or a snapshot taken by a friend – the important thing is that the picture should show the result of their efforts. As well as appreciating the personal gesture, the person will find the picture useful, adding it to their existing album in which they show future brides the style of their work.

Friends locally, perhaps those who have hosted house parties or dinner parties, could be offered a flower arrangement from one of the tables. Your parents shouldn't feel they must denude the house of flowers in order to express their thanks to people. But if there is an excess, the giving of flowers solves the problem as well as being a welcome gesture.

PARENTS AND IN-LAWS

It is easy to take the hard work of the people we love most for granted. Your mother and father, for example, have been doing things for you all your life, and they may have loved every moment of the wedding organisation. But habit and their enjoyment are not reasons why you should not show them how grateful you are for their contribution to the success and happiness of your wedding day. Stop and tell them so, and, in addition, give your mother a bunch or bouquet of her favourite flowers either on the day or the day before your marriage. Alternatively, your fiancé could give your mother flowers, and you could send your mother-in-law a bouquet, or arrange for it to be waiting at her hotel.

CHRONOLOGICAL CHECKLISTS

STAGE 1 CHECKLIST

Operates soon after you become engaged; starting about six months and not less than three months before the wedding. Ignore the points which don't apply to your arrangements.

◇ Announce engagement, personally and in the newspapers

◇ Equip yourself with stationery and stamps for replying to letters of congratulation

◇ Research possible dates for the wedding with your family and your fiancé's, as well as any professionals you want to be involved

◇ Decide where you would like to be married and visit the minister or officiant to discuss religious preparations, any necessity for a licence or other formalities, and to discuss possible alternative dates and times of day

◇ Establish what documentation you need and make sure you understand the ecclesiastical preliminaries such as the calling of banns

◇ When a date has been decided, inform the minister and members of the family which of the alternatives you have chosen

◇ Have a good look around the church and ask the minister about the altar cloth and vestments and any special carpet usually used for weddings or particular to the season when you are getting married. Make a note of the colours and bear them in mind when planning your wedding, as they will affect your choice of flowers

◇ Equip yourselves with a copy of the service and read it through together so you know exactly what's involved

◇ Discuss your marriage service with the minister or officiant. Decide roughly what order of service you would like, including music, hymns and lessons

◇ Discuss music with the organist. Choose specific pieces of music and decide who you would like to play/sing it. Research costs and book musicians

◇ Register-office wedding: take relevant documents to the registrar not more than three months or six months before the wedding (ring local office to check the current limit, when you become engaged) as the date cannot be set before this

◇ Discuss a budget with your parents and decide who is to pay for what. Consider offers of help from your fiancé's parents and others

◇ Decide time of wedding, how many people are to be invited, and format of celebrations to follow – stand-up reception, meal, dancing, entertainment, etc., having looked into the costs

◇ Decide upon the location for reception/party and book it

◇ Decide upon the style of the wedding, your dress and the reception, including colours

◇ Research costs and style of printers for the invitations. Discuss format, typeface, etc., with printer you have chosen. Give him correct wording and order invitations and any other stationery. Check the proof slowly and carefully and give it to someone else to read as a fresh eye can often spot mistakes you have missed. Go over corrections with printer and give the go-ahead for printing

◇ If you are having your reception/party at home, perhaps in a marquee, check with the electricity board that there is sufficient power for lighting, etc.

◇ Discuss power supply access and other technical requirements with marquee company, caterer and band

◇ Research different food, drink and caterers. Examine estimates closely for details like the cost of a meal for the staff who serve your meal, and the inclusion of staff, cutlery, crockery, glasses, etc. Book the caterers you choose

◇ If the celebrations are to include entertainment – band, disco, fireworks, etc. – research and book these

◇ Decide who is going to make and ice the wedding cake and discuss recipes, shapes and decorations. If you are making the cake yourself, plan a timetable for buying ingredients, cooking and icing it. If someone else is making the cake, order it

◇ Research florists and the types of flowers you envisage for yourself, the church and reception. Book florists

◇ If there are other weddings in the church on the same day, liaise with the other brides about flowers and costs.

◇ Discuss photographs and/or video in church with the minister and if he approves, discuss the positioning of the camera so it causes the least distraction to him, you and the congregation

◇ Research a photographer and video cameraman and book them (see page 56)

◇ Research hire cars or other vehicles and book them

◇ Plan any parts of the wedding which you are doing yourself such as dressmaking or cooking the food for the reception (see page 190)

◇ Choose your attendants, and your fiancé his best man

◇ Get your attendants, or their parents, to supply you with a complete list of measurements, sizes and likely rates of growth (if they are children)

◇ Decide whether your dress is to be bought, borrowed, made or hired and research styles, fabrics and accessories

◇ Consider what attendants are to wear

◇ Choose dresses (buy them, book them, etc.) and arrange fittings as necessary, for you and your attendants

◇ Decide upon the style of your veil

◇ Have your and your bridesmaids' shoes dyed as soon as you have decided on the fabric and colour

◇ Research possible stores and shops for your wedding lists, decide (with your fiancé) what you do and don't want

◇ Buy a book and numbered stickers, etc., to enable you to keep a full record of presents received and thanked for (see page 170)

◇ Write or type a sheet of details about your gift lists

◇ Make appointments to see doctor, dentist, lawyer or any other professionals

◇ Discuss your honeymoon. Research possibilities and book your choice

STAGE 2 CHECKLIST

Operates between three months and six weeks before the wedding, depending on when you began 'Stage 1'. Ignore the points which don't apply to your arrangements.

◇ Go over 'Stage 1 Checklist' and do anything overlooked

◇ Buy wedding ring(s) and send it/them to be engraved

◇ Finalise details about the order of service. Give it to the officiant and ask him to check that there are no mistakes

◇ Order service sheets from printer. Check proofs slowly and carefully and give them to someone else to read as a fresh eye can often spot mistakes you have missed. Go over corrections with printer and give the go-ahead for printing

◇ Ask the person who is to propose the first toast – traditionally your father or a family friend who has known you for a long time

◇ Keep a careful record of presents received, liaising regularly with your parents and fiancé. Decide with your fiancé which of you is going to write thank-you letters for which presents

◇ Research a possible registered childminder or other responsible person to run a crèche during the wedding service. Book the person and invite them to your parents' home or crèche location so they can familiarise themselves with surroundings and facilities. Discuss the number and ages of babies and children involved, and provision of biscuits, squash, toys, etc.

◇ Consider security at home on the day of the wedding if the house is to be left empty (weddings and funerals are notorious times for burglaries). Inform local police and, if necessary, book a security guard

◇ Ask for any help you would like from friends and relations. If they are unable to help or lend things, find alternatives

◇ Make a record of all friends who have volunteered to give house or dinner parties, and recruit others as necessary

◇ Prepare a note about house and dinner parties to go out with the invitations, alongside information about hotels

◇ Compile information about local hotels for guests travelling some distance, and make advance block bookings

◇ If taking your husband's name, get forms for post-dated passport and inform bank, tax office, etc. of forthcoming name change and date of marriage

◇ Bake the cake, if you are doing this yourself

◇ Buy shoes and other accessories for you and bridesmaids/attendants

◇ Decide upon and, if necessary, buy going-away clothes, hat and shoes

◇ Check your mother's progress on her clothes and hat

◇ Photocopy relevant directions and maps with all locations clearly marked. Send them to florist, caterer, car-hire firm, musicians etc.

◇ Check car-parking arrangements at church and reception

◇ Draw up guest list and cut it down to size. Apologise to friends and relatives who are below the line (if and when you see them)

◇ Begin addressing envelopes. Send all invitations at same time, about six weeks before the wedding, with directions, maps and hotel/house party information

◇ Keep a careful record of acceptances and refusals

◇ Allocate guests to house parties and dinner parties and write to both hosts and guests with details. Ask guests to contact their hosts for directions, etc.

◇ With your fiancé, compile a list of whom you would like to appear in which group photographs. Send copies to the photographer and best man, with family trees for your and your fiancé's families. If you have asked a relative to help marshal people for photos, send a copy to him or her too

◇ Discuss presents for the attendants with your fiancé; choose, buy and wrap them

◇ Write thank-you letters for gifts received

◇ Go to church to hear the banns read. See the minister or officiant, if he would like you to and you haven't already done so, to discuss the undertaking of marriage and arrange any final details

◇ Arrange the wedding rehearsal with the officiant and notify everyone you would like to be there (usually you and your fiancé, best man, attendants)

◇ Check the groom and best man have organised their wedding clothes

◇ Shop for any honeymoon clothes or equipment necessary

◇ Make final apppointments for hair, nails, etc., or arrange for relevant professionals to come to your home on the day of your wedding

◇ Rehearse wearing veil with hair arranged as for wedding day

◇ Confirm details of bridesmaids' appearance such as hair cut and jewellery

◇ Organise (or enrol chief bridesmaid to arrange) a celebration for a few close friends. Usually the sexes have their own evening or weekend party sometime in the weeks before the wedding. Decide what sort of event you want and who to invite. The best man should do the same for your fiancé

STAGE 3 CHECKLIST

Operates three or four weeks running up to the days immediately before the wedding day. Ignore the points which don't apply to your arrangements.

◇ Go over 'Stage 2 Checklist' and do anything overlooked

◇ Check groom has Certificate of Banns or other documentation in his possession or organised. Check he has tickets, etc. for honeymoon if you don't

◇ Telephone florist, caterer, cars and transport, photographer, musicians, etc. and make sure they have the correct brief, down to small details like who is delivering bouquets and buttonholes when and to where

◇ Start drawing up table plan for reception

◇ Have any cars involved serviced, including the going-away car. Make sure they are thoroughly cleaned inside and out and filled with petrol, oil and windscreen-washing fluid, a day or two before the wedding

◇ Check that your fiancé has asked ushers, including at least one from amongst your family and friends

◇ Brief best man and chief bridesmaid, or a relative, about removing your and your fiancé's wedding clothes from the reception location after you have changed to go away on your honeymoon

◇ If you have relatives coming from abroad, are having a marquee at home, or simply if you feel it would help smooth organisation, make a timetable of who is where and doing what in the last week before the wedding and circulate this to everyone appropriate

◇ Decide who is to do what and be where on the day of the wedding. Draw up a timetable and circulate it to everyone concerned

◇ Have your hair cut and check the groom and best man are having theirs cut

◇ Make a list of names, addresses and telephone numbers of important people – you and your fiancé, your and his parents, the officiant, organist or musicians, best man, chief bridesmaid, reception location, caterer, etc. and circulate to everyone appropriate on the list so that they all feel 'in the picture' and have the information in case of queries or an emergency

◇ Decide if you want to make a speech at the reception. Compile a list of people you would like your fiancé to thank in his speech (and you in yours if you plan to make one)

◇ Telephone guests who have not replied to the invitation, starting about a week before the wedding

◇ Confirm guest numbers (including small children in separate room and with special menu, and anyone else with a special diet) with the caterer on the date he/she has told you he/she needs them

◇ Decorate the cake

◇ Draw up seating plans for the church (your family) and reception (everyone). Get your fiancé to make a plan for his front pews. Make photocopies of church plan for ushers

◇ Order flowers to be delivered to your mother and mother-in-law on the day of or day before the wedding

◇ Do a practice run from your home to the church, driving slowly, and note the time it takes

◇ Make signs saying 'COATS', 'LOOS', 'LADIES', 'GENTLEMEN', 'PARTY', 'PARKING' with arrows pointing in the right directions

◇ Have manicure

◇ Pack honeymoon suitcase and arrange for it to be delivered, with your going-away clothes, to the place where you will be changing

◇ Check progress of reception arrangements including display of seating plan

◇ Position table numbers and place cards on tables at the reception

◇ Place name tags on front pews of church in accordance with seating plan

◇ Attend rehearsal on the eve of the wedding and make sure you understand the moves

◇ At the rehearsal, give the best man copies of your church seating plan to distribute to the ushers

◇ If guests are coming to your parents' house or if the reception is being held at a village or school hall, check there are plenty of towels, wastepaper baskets, bars of soap and rolls of lavatory paper in the loos

◇ Once you have made up on your wedding day, someone should take your make-up and spongebag to the place where you will change to go away on honeymoon. Arrange who will do this for you

◇ Have an early night, if possible, on the eve of the wedding

FINAL CHECKLIST

◇ The later the wedding, the longer you should try to sleep in

◇ Have a long (but not too long), relaxing bath

◇ Eat a good breakfast – you may not have time or be too nervous for lunch if it's an afternoon wedding

◇ Check that bouquets, head-dresses, buttonholes, etc. have been delivered or are on their way

◇ Put up signs with arrows for lavatories and parking

◇ Give your attendants their presents

◇ Check that none of your attendants is wearing a watch or jewellery which spoils their appearance, and remember to take off your own everyday watch

◇ Transfer your engagement ring to your right hand (same finger)

◇ Don't drink much fluid in the hours immediately before the service and, ideally, avoid alcohol

◇ Relax and enjoy yourself!

PHOTOGRAPHIC CREDITS

Page 1 Donna De Mari: p.2 Richard Imrie: p.3 Michael Woolley: p.5–7 Michael Woolley: p.10 Vicky Ceelan: p.12 Tim Bret-Day: p.13 Steve Lovi: p.14 Carl Bengtsson: p.15 Donna De Mari: p.16 Alan Fandall: p.21 Sandra Lousada: p.22–3 Donna De Mari: p.26 Jonathon Root: p.27 Jennifer Beeston (top), Ian Stratton (below): p.28 Emily Anderson: p.30 Donna De Mari: p.31 Sandra Lousada: p.32 Donna De Mari: p.35 Donna De Mari: p.37 Tim Bret-Day: p.38 Michael Woolley: p.39 Nic Tucker: p.42 Donna De Mari: p.54 Stuart Nicol: p.58 Jeremy Enness: p.59 Theodore Fleming: p.60 Donna De Mari: p.61 Jennifer Beeston: p.62 Donna De Mari: p.67 Jeremy Enness: p.68 Graham Harrison: p.69 Mark Tillier: p.72 not known: p.74 Stuart Nicol: p.75 Jennifer Beeston: p.76 Ian Stratton: p.78–9 Nancy Durrell McKenna: p.80 Stuart Nicol (top left and below), Jeremy Enness (top right): p.84–5 Polly Wreford: p.86–7 Ian Stratton: p.88–9 Ben Rice: p.90–1 Tim Bret-Day: p.92 Stuart Nicol: p.93 Polly Wreford: p.96 Calliope Clarke: p.100–3 Sandra Lousada: p.104–6 Michael Woolley: p.107 Stefano Massimo (top centre), Michael Woolley (all others): p.108–9 Andrea Alberts: (top left and centre), Ian Stratton (top right), Calliope Clarke (below left and right): p.110 Calliope Clarke: p.111 Calliope Clarke (main picture), Donna De Mari (top right): p.112 Sandra Lousada: p.113 Michael Woolley: p.114 Nick Briggs: p.115 Jennifer Beeston (top right), Nick Briggs (all others): p.116 Michael Woolley: p.117 Polly Wreford (top right), Stefan Massimo (all others): p.118 Calliope Clarke: p.119 Nick Briggs (top left and right), Avi Meroz (below left), Tierney Gearon (below right): p.120 Stevie Hughes: p.121 Jeremy Enness (top left and right, and below left), Neil Kirk (below right): p.122–3 Michael Woolley: p.124 Sandra Lousada: p.125 Jeremy Enness: p.126 Sandra Lousada (top left), Jennifer Beeston (centre), Jean Pierre Masclet (top right), Calliope Clarke (below left), Jeremy Enness (below right): p.127 Ian Stratton: p.128 Tim Bret-Day (left), Calliope Clarke (top right), Stuart Nicol (below): p.129 Theodore Wood (top left), Jean Pierre Masclet (top right), Sandra Lousada (below): p.130 Ian Stratton (top centre), Tim Bret-Day (top left), Jeremy Enness (below right), Jean Pierre Masclet (centre and below left): p.131 Michael Woolley: p.132 Tim Bret-Day: p.133 Richard Imrie: p.134 Sandra Lousada: p.136 Donna De Mari: p.137 Jeremy Enness (top left), Stuart Nicol (top centre), Ian Stratton (top and below right), Donna De Mari (below left): p.138 Sandra Lousada: p.139 Jennifer Beeston (top left and right), Jeremy Enness (below left), Ian Stratton (below right): p.140 Ian Stratton (top and below left), Theodore Wood (below right): p.141 Theodore Wood (top left), Ian Stratton (top centre), Nick Tucker (top right), Philip Webb (below left), Ben Rice (below right): p.142 Nick Briggs: p.143 Michael Woolley (top left), Nick Briggs (top right), Philip Webb (below left and right): p.144 Ian Stratton (top left), Tim Bret-Day (top right), Sandra Lousada (below left), Emily Anderson (below right): p.145 Jennifer Beeston: p.146 Sandra Lousada: p.148 Jeremy Enness (top left), Polly Wreford (top centre), Jennifer Beeston (top right), Jeremy Enness (below left and right): p.149 Jennifer Beeston: p.150 Michael Woolley: p.151 Jeremy Enness: p.152 Theodore Wood (top left and centre), Ian Stratton (top right and below): p.153 Jeremy Enness (top left), Ian Stratton (top right), Emily Anderson (below left), Donna De Mari (below right): p.154 Ian Stratton (top left), Polly Wreford (top right), Jeremy Enness (below): p.155–6 Jeremy Enness: p.157 Polly Wreford: p.158 Ian Stratton: p.159 Jeremy Enness (top left and centre), Ian Stratton (top right and below left): p.160 Jennifer Beeston (top left), P. Wren (top right), Theodore Wood (below): p.161 Jennifer Beeston (top left and centre left), Jeremy Enness (top right), Emily Anderson (below): p.162 Donna De Mari: p.164 Nick Briggs: p.165 Jennifer Beeston: p.166 Sandra Lousada: p.167 Jennifer Beeston: p.169 Steve Lovi: p.172 Donna De Mari: p.177 Jeremy Enness: p.178 Steve Kibble: p.179 Ian Stratton (left), Jennifer Beeston (centre), Emily Anderson (right): p.180 Mark Tillier (left), Emily Anderson (top right), Ben Rice (centre left), Jeremy Enness (centre right), Ian Stratton (below): p.181 Ian Stratton (top left), Jennifer Beeston (top right), Emily Anderson (below): p.182 Ian Stratton: p.183 David Montgomery: p.184 Donna De Mari: p.186 Jennifer Beeston: p.187 Jeremy Enness (top centre), Ian Stratton (all others): p.190 Donna De Mari: p.191 Peter Myers: p.192 Jeremy Enness: p.193 Jennifer Beeston: p.196 Donna De Mari: p.197 Ian Stratton: p.198 Jennifer Beeston: p.199 Emily Anderson: p.200 Simon Bottomley: p.202 Bermuda Tourist Board.

The publishers have made every effort to contact the photographers listed above, and all those people who appear in the photographs, but in some cases this has not been possible and we would like to apologise if this has caused any inconvenience.

The publishers would also like to thank the following for permission to use illustrations: p.52 Jean Halperin (Jewish wedding invitation) and Wren Press.

INDEX